OPERATION PINBALL

Ivan Hickman

To Bobbie,
whose frequent reminders helped
mend my lethargic ways.

First published in 1990 by Motorbooks International Publishers & Wholesalers, P O Box 2, 729 Prospect Avenue, Osceola, WI 54020 USA

Library of Congress Cataloging-in-Publication Data
Hickman, Ivan.
Operation Pinball / Ivan Hickman.
p. cm.
ISBN 0-87938-472-7
1. World War, 1939-45—Aerial operations, American.
2. Aerial gunnery—History. I. Title.
D790.H54 1990 90-5945
940.54'4973—dc20 CIP

On the front cover: RP-63C-2s warm up their engines at Bell's Niagara, New York, aircraft factory. *E. F. Furler, Jr.*

On the back cover: Gunnery training as it was before the pinball: the student gunner fires a .30 caliber machine gun at a target towed by another AT-6. *US Air Force*

Author photo: Author Ivan Hickman at the controls (also in back) of a Cessna 340.

Printed and bound in the United States of America

Contents

Preface

To an observer on the ground, the two aircraft high above represented just another episode in the continuing air warfare that proliferated in many parts of the world in the early months of 1945. The larger of the two, a four-engined bomber, lumbered along, seemingly unperturbed by the frantic attacks of a tiny fighter, responding almost casually with chattering machine gun fire to each pass.

The contest came to an end when the fighter pilot noticed an ominous increase in engine coolant temperature. Wasting little time he broke off the duel and headed for home. Reacting to a radio call from his erstwhile opponent, he began a slow turn and, glancing back, noticed a distinct trail of vapor or smoke. At the same time he recognized the pungent odor of ethylene glycol fumes in the cockpit.

The fighter pilot felt himself losing consciousness and now, definitely concerned, managed to move the engine mixture control to idle cutoff and kill the overheated power plant.

He regained his senses a moment later and, still somewhat groggy, glanced at his altimeter. In a right-hand spiral, his aircraft was descending through 5,000 feet, perilously close to the mountainous terrain. He managed to level his airplane and, unfastening his restraining harness, bailed out. How quickly it all had happened, the pilot thought as his mind began to clear. Floating down with the parachute canopy billowing out above, he recapped the strange occurrence. Only one thing could have caused the mishap, he concluded: a bullet from his enemy's machine gun must have penetrated a coolant radiator.

The fighter pilot survived with some injuries and personnel from his home base soon rescued him. This incident, like several others, occurred on an irregular basis during the final year of the conflict we remember as World War II. Like all of them, this one varied significantly from combat still raging in various theaters of war around the globe.

First, these two aircraft displayed identical US Army Air Force markings and crewmen of both contesting aircraft served in the same military service. Second, the attacking fighter never fired on his adversary, very strange indeed for an aircraft in aerial combat. Third, the fighter was painted a bright orange, a color never envisioned in that day and age for wartime use. Finally, the action took place within the continental limits of the United States over a barren, mountainous desert area near Indian Springs, north of Las Vegas, Nevada.

The two airplanes had been engaged in the little-known frangible bullet program, the ultimate phase of World War II flexible gunnery training. This accident became the first—but by no means the last—to occur during the few months this imaginative concept was in being.

How did it all come about? It wasn't easy, as we shall see, but it provides a fascinating insight into high-level bumbling and low-level ineptitude, occasionally interspersed with instances of inspired performance by dedicated, visionary individuals. The concept became a reality because a few men refused to succumb to traditionally inflexible attitudes of "chairborne" military autocrats.

Foreword

The initial impetus for my decision to write about frangible bullet training came from John Szabo of Riverside, California, who identifies himself as a researcher of Kingman Army Air Field and World War II aircraft scrapping operations. John had written to one of the commercial flying magazines, soliciting contacts with people who had served at Kingman during World War II. He was contemplating a history of that short-lived installation, and I responded. I informed him that I spent almost two years there and was ready to assist in whatever way I could.

When I told John about my experiences with the frangible bullet (popularly remembered as "pinball") training program, he encouraged me to write a book. This was early in 1982 and I began seeking assistance. I was fortunate in meeting Dwayne Reed, chief of the special collections division at the United States Air Force Academy Library, and he has been instrumental in directing my research efforts. He acquainted me with the Albert F. Simpson (now renamed USAF) Historical Research Center at Maxwell Air Force Base, Montgomery, Alabama, which is recognized today as the semi-official archives of the US Air Force. While trying to decide how to approach the problem of researching the center's massive files, a true bonanza fell into my lap.

C. J. Rieman was a P–38 pilot in the South Pacific during World War II who flew with Charles Lindbergh on some of the missions in which the Lone Eagle participated. C. J. and I became friends through our mutual interests when I worked for the *Colorado Springs Sun* in the early seventies covering, among other things, local aviation news. C. J. really started this project by showing to me the August 1976 *Air Force* magazine. In it he had found an article called "The Texas Pinball Machine" by Capt. John D. Edgar. Edgar wrote the story while attending the Air Command and Staff School at Maxwell Air Force Base, and assuming that he had obtained his material from the Albert F. Simpson Historical Research Center, I set out to locate Edgar.

Edgar, by 1982 a lieutenant colonel, was stationed at Ft. Belvoir, Virginia. I wrote to him, outlining my project, and requested a bibliography of his research material. From previous correspondence with the Albert F. Simpson Historical Research Center, I learned that microfilm copies of file material were available. Such a list would enable me to properly identify and order what I needed.

Col. Edgar responded, providing not only a list of the material he had used, but also copies of the original documents themselves. I thus obtained, with very little effort on my part, a comprehensive file of technical and historical data upon which I have drawn extensively in preparing this work. At Dwayne Reed's suggestion and with permission from Col. Edgar, I have donated all this research material to the United States Air Force Academy. It now reposes in the academy library's special collections division.

At the time I first contacted Edgar, I had decided to extend my efforts to encompass a history of United States Army flexible gunnery training, from its inception to the end of World War II. This would provide an understanding and lead-in to the later chapters covering the primary subject of the frangible bullet. I should point out that while the Army and Navy collaborated in many areas of flexible gunnery training, the Navy did not incorporate the frangible bullet concept into its training curricula, and except for occasional references in the body of this work, I have excluded the Navy from consideration. This is not to infer, by any means, that our naval service lagged in flexible gunnery training. On the contrary, Navy aerial gunners performed admirably in the war, and I do not presume to denigrate their efforts.

I have written in the third person, although I share, to a large extent, the many personal experiences narrated herein. I have, therefore, exercised a journalistic prerogative by adding an occasional sidebar following certain chapters to amplify, with my comments, the subject under discussion. I solicited, through various publications, inputs from persons with knowledge of the frangible bullet training program and the response has been gratifying. I now have an extensive file of letters and taped conversations, the contents of which are interspersed throughout the book.

Operation Pinball covers up to the cessation of hostilities in 1945, although the final chapter deals with some minor efforts of the Strategic Air Command to employ the frangible bullet in some of their postwar training programs. For all intents and purposes, 1945 marked the end of flexible gunnery training as we knew it long ago. The introduction of swifter, jet-powered aircraft brought new and sophisticated dimensions to the problem of defending large, weapons-carrying warplanes. The treatment of modern training methods properly belongs in a distinctly separate work and I leave this to others.

Although the modern Air Force did not achieve a separate distinction until the aviation function broke away from the Army in 1947, I have used the term "Air Force" interchangeably with Army Air Corps and Army Air Forces throughout the book. In addition, the reader will find "pinball" in lower case and without quotation marks in referring to the frangible bullet program.

Ivan Hickman
Colorado Springs, Colorado

Acknowledgments

Many fine people assisted, in various capacities, in finalizing *Operation Pinball*. I find it difficult to properly recognize them all; I can only try. We share a common interest in World War II military history, and most of my correspondents participated in some fashion in the pinball program. Some are avid military aviation enthusiasts, and their contributions were no less valuable than those who wrote of their wartime experiences. They represent a bona fide cross section of modern society; some are retired military, others represent academia in one form or another. All of them were valuable to me and I have made many friends in the process.

Lt. Colonel John D. Edgar was a surrogate researcher as I documented in the Foreword. To him, especially, I owe an outstanding debt of gratitude. Special thanks also to Dwayne Reed who led me by the hand wondering, I suspect, just how one as green and naive as I initially appeared could ever consummate a project like this. He referred me in the beginning to the excellent *Flexible Gunnery Training in the AAF*, an official Army history and the primary source of information contained in chapters 4 through 8. He encouraged and advised me, and gave me access to the voluminous files in the Special Collections Division of the Air Force Academy Library.

Edward F. Arbogast, Jr., a gunnery student at Laredo during the war and a retired high school English teacher, assisted with my final rewrite and kept my grammar and syntax moderately on track. He and I corresponded frequently, and more than once I mailed the entire manuscript to him for his pertinent observations and recommendations. His inputs comprise a generous part of the book and I am grateful for his assistance.

I'm also indebted to Ernest R. (Ernie) McDowell of Chicago, another faithful correspondent whose advice proved most helpful. The author of a number of excellent books on World War II military aircraft, Ernie edited my first rewrite and provided the in-depth review of turrets in chapter 8. He loaned me a number of photos from his extensive file, copies of which I have freely utilized, and for the use of which I'm truly grateful.

E. F. (Ed) Furler, Jr., authored a fine series of articles on the Bell fighters which appeared in *Air Classics* magazine. I first corresponded with Ed back in 1974 and he has helped me immensely with a number of still photos and much sound advice. I soon found out that he knew more about the P-39 than I did . . . and I, unlike Ed, *flew* the machines. Much the same applies to Randall Dunkley, too young to have participated in World War II but a true aviation buff nonetheless. We have been in regular contact for some time. He is an authority on the Indian Springs airfield of bygone days and has provided information on the Airacobra which, I confess, I never knew or had since forgotten.

I mentioned John Szabo in the Foreword. He has also kept in touch and has provided much information on the old Kingman Army Air Field. And Rick Sherry, a fellow Colorado Springs resident and a contributor to various publications, was the first to examine a rough draft of this work. I have benefited from his constructive criticisms.

I'm grateful to Beaufort Technical College of Beaufort, South Carolina, for a fine word processing course I took during a winter sojourn down there in 1984–85. I had access to the school's IBM computers in the classroom lab during off-class hours, and it was there I produced my first draft. And I profited from the efforts of an excellent instructor, Jeynean Briley. She taught me how to use the processor and gave me a genuine appreciation of this modern electronic marvel, a real learning experience.

Even my relatives got into the act. My daughter-in-law, an accomplished typist and ultimately a competent word processor operator, did many drafts on my son's Apple IIc, interfaced with a slow daisy wheel printer. My thanks to her. My nephew, Earl G. Hickman, Jr., a remarkably knowledgeable young man who is an expert with small-bore rifles, obtained a box of frangible rounds from his friend, Cal Johnson. He presented them to me and I express my appreciation to him.

Among my most cherished mementos is a copy of a pilot's manual for the P-63C, the Dash One, given to me by Bob Corson. When it arrived I leafed through it, nostalgia growing by leaps and bounds, after which I informed my wife I knew I could once again climb into that beautiful bird and fly it, just as if those forty-some odd years had not elapsed. I'll remember Bob for his contribution.

I'd be derelict if I failed to mention three more fine people. Ursula Bird, mentioned briefly in chapter 1, checked and corrected the few German words I used. Walter Musciano, author of the superlative *Messerschmitt Aces* from which I borrowed extensively, provided some of the German *Experten* photos, and John Campbell also assisted in illustrating the book's initial chapter.

In addition to the many correspondents who wrote and are recognized in the body of this book, I'm obliged to name some others who provided advice and assistance. They are: Charles B. Badgett, Charles Cook, Olin Brown, Wayne L. Daniel, Merrell C. Dennard, Kenneth Dowd, Al Foss, Eugene E. Fucci, John J. Kropenick, Edomer Lynch, James D. Mehegan, Jr., David Menard, Jay Miller, T. V. Murphy, Jim Pulliam, William H. Roden, Eugene Safan, Richard Tausing, Arthur N. White, David W. Williams and Erroll L. Williams.

Introduction

Many years have passed since I last climbed into the cockpit of a World War II fighter and there are many things I no longer remember. One part of my military career remains crystal clear, however: the final year of the war that witnessed the culmination of years of planning and frustration, the year that saw the implementation of a whole new concept of training, the frangible bullet flexible gunnery training program.

My fellow pilots and I were fortunate, in a way, in having a plethora of handy forced landing sites—the many dry lakes dotting the mountainous terrain near my last World War II station, Indian Springs, Nevada. And some of us made good use of them. I always wondered about pilots who operated over less friendly territory, such as the Everglades in Florida or over coastal waters. Accidents happened in those areas, too, and there are reports of pilots bailing out when trouble with the P-63 developed. The early models were beset with engine malfunctions that caused some concern. These were corrected, as we shall see.

But this is a story of accomplishment . . . and there was plenty of that in that long-remembered pinball program. This is the story of a lower-ranking officer and a farsighted college professor who envisioned a dream and saw it through to fruition.

This is the story of some apprehensive young men who engaged in a strange type of combat without the attendant combat emoluments. These were young men who swallowed their fears and flew their missions, finding in the process that most of those fears were groundless.

This is a story of an innovative concept that, given sufficient time, would have proven of inestimable value to those who manned the guns of our immense bomber fleets. It's the story of time and circumstances which combined to thwart, in the final analysis, the ambitious expectations of a few dedicated planners. This is the story of the pinballs and the men who flew them.

The rude awakening

1

It's probably unfair to accuse the United States Air Force's Bomber Command of overconfidence in its first forays into the European air war. There was this obvious cockiness, however . . . and there appeared to be good reason. After all, we did have those magnificent B-17s and B-24s bristling with our fantastic .50 caliber machine guns, the armament that was to have made our bombers impervious to enemy fighters. Or so we were told.

It didn't take long to learn that modern air warfare wasn't all that simple. We also learned that the .50 caliber, superior weapon that it was, needed a cool head with extensive, realistic training to aim it properly.

Following the Japanese attack on Pearl Harbor, we had our heavy bombers out prepared for action, although in insufficient numbers and in somewhat disorganized fashion. We were completely unprepared for the kind of total warfare in which we were about to engage.

During the entire war, the Pacific combat zone was considered secondary in importance to the European theater, and aerial gunnery in the Pacific did not pose the same problems we encountered against the Germans. General Kenney, undoubtedly the most imaginative and resourceful of our World War II aerial commanders, managed his limited resources remarkably well. The wide expanses of the Pacific dictated entirely different tactics than those employed in Europe, and Kenney tried to always provide fighter escort for his comparatively minuscule bomber forces. He was forced out of necessity to use a preponderance of medium bombers, primarily B-25s. Japanese fighters, as proficient as Nipponese pilots were in the beginning, did infinitesimal damage compared to that inflicted by the German *Jagdwaffe* in Europe. (Germans called their fighter pilots "hunters." The German word for hunter is *Jaeger*; *Waffe*, in German, means "weapon" or "arm." Hence, *Luftwaffe* represents the German air weapon or arm, and *Jagdwaffe*, loosely interpreted, means "fighter weapon" or "arm." *Jagd* is used in many forms, among them *Jagdflieger*, the term we equate with "fighter pilot.")

So it was the bombing missions in Europe that highlighted our deficiencies in aerial gunnery. From the first tentative strike against Nazi objectives, the modest raid by twelve B-17s of the newly formed Eighth Air

The B-24 was the bomber workhorse of the USAAF during World War II. Approximately 18,000 of the Convair-designed Liberators were built, more than any other type four-engined bomber, including the B-17. Note the slim, high-aspect ratio wing. Called the Davis after its designer, it was really a form of the laminar and was responsible for the aircraft's fine performance. Fred C. Dickey, Jr., via Ernest R. McDowell

Force against the marshaling yards at Rouen-Sotteville, France, on August 17, 1942, to the massive 1,000-plane forays deep into the heart of Germany toward the end of the war, we learned—but we learned the hard way.

In view of our continuing insistence that bombing raids be conducted during daylight hours with our aircraft's defensive firepower our only protection, it's ironic indeed that this diminutive force was escorted to the target area by four Royal Air Force squadrons of Spitfire IX fighters. Five squadrons picked up the bombers on their return and escorted them back to their base in England. It means that some sixty fighters escorted twelve bombers in and seventy-five protected them on their way out, a far cry from that future day when bombers would consistently outnumber their "little friends."

Of course, this was really a feeling-out raid, one that was not expected to produce extensive damage. It was designed to give the planners an opportunity to assess the validity of bombing techniques and provide experience for the crews. The force dropped slightly more than eighteen tons of bombs from an altitude of 23,000 feet. Records reflect that approximately half the bomb loads fell in the target area. Anti-aircraft fire slightly damaged two of the B-17s, and three Messerschmitt Bf 109 fighters attacked the formation without result. Ironically, the only injury sustained by crew members was caused on the return when a pigeon smashed against the plexiglass nose of one of the bombers, inflicting minor cuts to the bombardier and navigator from showering particles.

The Sotteville marshaling yard in Rouen contained a large locomotive depot (known in the United States as a roundhouse) and many railroad repair shops. Nothing was seriously damaged, and rail traffic was only slightly interrupted. Gunners did have the opportunity to fire their weapons, and they contributed to much of the misplaced euphoria that set in following the raid. The German fighter attacks were somewhat tentative, not at all the ferocious kind that characterized later combat when the heart of Germany was attacked. It didn't take long for the *Jagdflieger* to become acquainted with this strange and formidable new aircraft, and the losses we suffered later on testifies to the skill and daring of this highly motivated group of fighting men. It should also be noted in passing that none of the 144 machine guns carried by the twelve B-17s caused any damage to the attacking fighters.

W. W. (Ike) Adamson, a veteran of twenty-eight missions in B-17s with the Eighth Air Force, has strong opinions about his gunnery training. The pinball program was unknown to him when he went overseas in 1943. He ruefully recalls, "Our training was based on the theory of fighters making classic 'pursuit curve' attacks from the rear of the bomber formation. This was, for the most part, exactly opposite to the training required for the head-on attacks the Luftwaffe began making early on.

"Most of the B-17 firepower was concentrated aft and manned by gunners well trained to repel fighters pressing their attacks on the rear quadrant of our formation," he recalls. "However, the forward defensive armament was (usually) manned by officer-rated navigators and bombardiers, many of whom had ignored [or been excused from] gunnery training, and in combat were tasked with the twelve o'clock level defensive cone of fire." Adamson notes that neither the Sperry upper nor lower ball turrets could cover this critical area during level flight.

Adamson points out another problem with the "attack from the rear" theory of training: "Assume the speed of the attacking fighter is 450 mph and the bomber speed is 200. When the fighter is attacking from the rear the bomber speed is subtracted from the fighter speed, giving a rate of closure of 250 mph. This gives the gunner ample time to set up the deflection on his iron ring and post sight, smoothly track and fire controlled bursts. Conversely, with a head-on attack the bomber speed is *added* to the attacking fighter speed and the rate of closure becomes 650 mph. One can readily see that this leaves very little time for anything but a short burst."

Adamson goes on to say that flexible gunnery school turret tracking exercises, "Jam Handy" simulator training, ground firing at moving targets and air-to-air firing at sleeve targets were all based on the slow rate of closure theory. He compares it to a baseball team, well-trained to hit only slow curve ball pitches, hitting against a fast ball pitcher.

When queried on whether pinball training would have helped, Adamson's answer is "Yes, Yes, a thousand times Yes!" It would have helped the nose gunners most," he maintains, "in the following ways: the flashing prop hub light (on the pinball fighter) would simulate the flashes of the Me-109 20 mm cannon during head-on passes; it would improve burst control, (helping to prevent) spraying the sky or shooting the letter "W" pattern; and it would have developed high-speed tracking and proper deflection techniques." (It should be noted that pinball training was restricted, in most cases, to curve of pursuit passes. However, it stands to reason that head-on passes would eventually have been used in the program once the necessity became apparent.)

Despite the priority given to the European theater, initial aircraft allocations were made to the Pacific where immediate action was required to prevent our complete annihilation. In addition, a few B-24s were sent to Egypt where the British were hard-pressed in the summer of 1942 at about the same time the Eighth Air Force was activated in Great Britain. The massive build-up began there with three groups of B-17s and three groups of fighters. One fighter group was comprised of P-38s and the other two, initially equipped with P-39s (already declared unfit for European air warfare), left their Airacobras behind and were provided ex-RAF Spitfires which they used for some time.

Early in 1942 the British began to prepare for the massive American military build-up that was coming. The Eighth Air Force was allocated a total of 127 airfields, installations and other facilities required to sustain what would eventually become the mightiest aerial fighting force the world had ever seen. And while the Training Command in the United States was feverishly preparing gunners to man the weapons of this growing fleet, General Eaker, first commanding general of the Eighth, and his staff were giving little thought to gunners, expecting the personnel sent to man the machines to be fully qualified. It was only later that the decision was made to include gunnery in bomber operational training programs.

From the first halting steps, the Eighth grew in gargantuan proportions. The Rouen raid involved a total of 160 American personnel; 2½ years later a mass attack in heavy bombers alone would involve more than 25,000 officers and men, the vast majority of them gunners.

The Eighth was by no means the only force in Europe. Following the Eighth in England came the Ninth 1½ years later out of North Africa, where it had operated in commendable fashion supporting the Allied invasion there in November of 1942. Later, when US forces were established on the European continent, the Fifteenth was activated in Italy. This force was to prove well nigh indispensable in coordinating attacks with the Eighth into the heart of Germany. The Twelfth Air Force, established in North Africa, was also oriented toward the heavy bomber. These four air forces complemented each other well and each required increasing numbers of gunners to man their weapons. The Eighth took the brunt of the casualties; this is the Heavy Bombardment force we remember and most readily associate with World War II.

The Rouen raid gave little warning that the Allied brass, who originally planned the aerial attacks against German targets, had seriously underestimated the fighting skill and dedication of the Luftwaffe. In addition, major mistakes were made in evaluating the capabilities of the Allied forces. It all contributed to the huge losses in aircraft and manpower Allied forces were to assume as their raids proliferated. It proved conclusively that gunners, given the training to which they were currently exposed, were incapable of protecting their aircraft without the assistance of escorting fighters. Make no mistake: the *Jagdwaffe* was a potent force, not to be taken lightly.

Charles J. Warth had a remarkable tour in B-24s. He flew out of Bengazi, Libya, in 1943 training for the Ploesti raid which came later. Warth missed that one when he was shot down over Foggia, Italy, on his twelfth mission and taken prisoner. He, along with a British commando, escaped after five weeks of captivity. He made his way to England by a roundabout route, whereupon he was returned to the United States.

Warth remembers his combat missions well. "Our B-24 Liberators were mostly 'D' models," he recalls,

A B-17G. Note the chin turret on the nose, one of the desperate measures to increase forward firepower. German fighter attacks increasingly came from dead ahead. Ernest R. McDowell

"equipped with a top turret operated by the engineer, a nose gun . . . which the bombardier would (man) after he dropped his bombs, and at the two hatch windows we had twin .50 caliber machine guns and a .50 caliber in the camera hatch. And, of course, there were the two in the tail turret.

"There was no heating system in the rear of the plane and very little in the front. The hatch windows were open at all times and the interior of the plane was always zero or below at altitudes of 18,000 to 24,000 feet, which is where we flew most of our missions.

"In combat there was no systematic firing control—if you saw an enemy plane, you shot at it if you thought it was within range (most of the time it wasn't). Our formations were tight and most of the time gunners from several ships were firing at the same target (there were quite a few of our own aircraft damaged or accidentally shot down by our own actions)."

Warth acknowledges that they were "flying in combat against the best squadrons that the Luftwaffe had. German planes and pilots were well maintained and trained, and their bases were well within reach of any of our missions at that time [1943]." Warth describes his first mission when they were hit by enemy action, resulting in the downing of one of the formation's B-24s, carrying a crew he had been with back in the States. He maintains that they were well trained to operate the planes and equipment available in the summer of 1943. He does not feel that more training would have helped in any way. "We were hit with the best Germany had," Warth concedes, "and we lost eight of our planes that . . . morning of August 16, 1943. Official records confirm we shot down twenty-seven of their planes [a remarkable score, in light of later statistics]."

Opinions of gunners ran the gamut from "Pinball training was great" to "It probably wouldn't have helped much." Archie Callahan had thirty missions in B-24s, all of them over Germany and against less-experienced *Jagdflieger* in the later stages of the war. He tells an interesting story:

"My experiences as a gunner were somewhat different than those of the men who first saw combat in the beginning of the air war in 1943. Those were the raids where you fought your way in to the target and all the way home [against the very best fighter pilots Germany had]. In those days American fighter protection was limited. Our fighters did not have the range to accompany the bombers on the deep penetration raids into Europe.

"My group went operational May 30, 1944, and by that time our fighters had increased their range to stay with the bombers all the way. This was particularly true when the P-51 became available. This is not to say that we had fighter protection on every mission, however. There weren't enough fighters to cover all the groups of bombers.

"As the war progressed, the Germans used many different tactics to stop our bombers. One such tactic was to form packs of fighters and hit the groups head-on. They would line up fifty or more planes and hit a group, wiping out a squadron in seconds, at times. During these attacks the forward gunners were helpless to stop the onslaught.

"During my period of combat, flak was our biggest worry. The B-24 flew much lower than the B-17 [some would dispute this] and was a prime target. We were at such a low altitude on the St. Lo mission that the Germans were using their 88s on their tanks to fire at us."

Callahan went through flexible gunnery school at a relatively early time and became involved with the pinball program on his return. His experience with pinball missions may not have been typical but he doesn't believe this training would have been beneficial. He

The twin-engined Messerschmitt Bf 110 proved a formidable adversary to our bomber formations over Germany and Italy. The "G" model had a 37 mm Flak 18 gun, two 20 mm cannons and three 7.9 mm machine guns firing forward. The 110 lost much of its effectiveness when Allied fighters began escorting bombers to the farthest reaches of Germany. It was particularly helpless against our P-51. Ernest R. McDowell

was particularly impressed with the Waller trainer which had a huge curved screen "on which were projected simulated fighter attacks. This was so realistic you could work up a real sweat fighting off enemy attacks."

Callahan was a tail gunner and remembers one interesting episode which had the effect of keeping him awake. "I know you are familiar with contrails," he writes. "I don't recall the particular mission but we were over Europe and on our way to the target, and the contrails were very dense. From my tail position I was entirely blind directly to the rear. The Germans knew this and had been flying in the contrails to sneak up from the rear. I had been alerted to this situation by our intelligence and my eyes were glued to the rear, staring into the thick cloud of vapor.

"Suddenly I saw a twin-engined, twin-tailed plane (Bf 110) rise up out of the mist and just as suddenly duck back down. He couldn't see any better than I and had to come up to spot his prey. It was easy to doze off on those long missions and, particularly, in the tail turret. The Germans were aware of this as they played cat and mouse. The second time he came up he had closed the distance between us and I wasn't taking any chances. I let go and fired directly down the contrail, watching the tracers burn into the mist. I don't know if I got any hits but he did a wingover and disappeared. I don't know who was more scared by the sudden blast of machine gun fire, the Germans or my own crew. One thing for sure, the enemy had run into a wide-awake tail gunner that day!"

In the spring of 1943 the Eighth Air Force was ready to assume its full share of the war against the German heartland. After recovering many of the aircraft diverted to North Africa, it now had some 500 bombers and could, at any time, put half of them in the air. Raids had become bolder since the Rouen-Sotteville escapade and aircraft losses, while causing some concern, were insufficient to induce planners to deviate from their cherished daylight precision bombing. P-47s entered combat in April and after some familiarization flights of minor importance, made their first escort mission on May 4 when the Eighth conducted a raid on Antwerp. This effort was typical of early Thunderbolt assistance. The big fighter, magnificent and effective as it was at altitude, was hampered by its relatively short range and, until large disposable drop tanks were developed, limited in its escort capability. The P-51, when it appeared upon the scene, changed all that but Bomber Command was not too worried at this time.

So the all-out American assault began and the new daylight threat caused the Germans to begin hasty transfers of fighter units from the Eastern and Mediterranean fronts. The increase in *Jagdwaffe* strength, containing as it did some of the premier fighter pilots of the Luftwaffe, was immediately made known. The Eighth was concentrating at this time on targets in northern Germany, and in a raid on Kiel and Bremen on June 13 lost twenty-six bombers, twenty-two of them from newly-arrived, inexperienced groups. Despite many claims of kills, little evidence exists that gunners did much damage to the German fighters. This was typical. It has been estimated that gunner kill claims were in error in the ratio of ten to one.

With the advent of fine summer weather, deeper penetrations into Germany were conducted and the intensity of German fighter opposition resulted in the loss of 128 bombers during the month of July. Gunners, however, believed they were downing an exorbitant number of the enemy, claiming a fantastic total of 545 kills in those thirty-one days. Actual German losses amounted to only forty aircraft. This disparity was caused primarily by the massed fire of multiple guns aimed at a single target, but the fact remains that gunners were just not getting the job done. The *Jagdflieger* were adopting new tactics, learning quickly that head-on passes, even at a closing rate of 600 mph, were getting better results because of the formations' reduced firepower to the front. The twin-engined Messerschmitt Bf 110, with its heavy offensive armament, was causing most of the damage. This continued until P-51s were able to escort the bomber formations all the way to their destinations. The Bf 110 proved particularly easy prey for the Mustang.

Subsequent to the tragic August 1, 1943, raid on Ploesti, Rumania, by 178 B-24s (three groups from the Eighth joined the Twelfth and Ninth in this attack), the most ambitious effort out of England came on August 17. This was the first anniversary of the initial B-17 raid on Europe and planners went all out selecting targets and routes. One division (approximately 320 aircraft) attacked the Messerschmitt factory at Regensburg, then continuing on, recovered at Twelfth and Ninth Air Force bases in North Africa. Another division was directed to the ball bearing factories at Schweinfurt. The German fighters mauled the two forces to the tune of sixty bombers downed, an unacceptable rate of attrition for a single day.

A further raid on ball bearing factories at Stuttgart cost us forty-five aircraft. This occurred on September 6, and we persisted on October 8 with a raid on Bremen. We lost another thirty aircraft there, with twenty-six more extensively damaged. Twenty-eight losses were incurred over Poland on October 9, and on the 19th we lost another thirty in an attack on Muenster. And we kept trying at Schweinfurt, losing sixty more on that "Black Thursday," October 17, 1943.

This raid, characterized by most knowledgeable historians as utter stupidity, gave ample reason to believe that our Bomber Command had not yet learned its lesson. Now it became increasingly evident that, confronted by *Jagdwaffe* professionals, the bombers could not perform their missions unescorted without incurring unacceptable losses in men and materiel. It was with extreme reluctance that the staff at Bomber Command decided that deep penetration forays would have to cease until adequate escort protection could be provided. Despite enormous claims to the contrary, gunners were downing insignificant numbers of enemy fighters and representatives from stateside commands

A B-17 with the name Hell's Angels *was first to complete a combat tour and was brought home to spur bond drives. Shown here is aircraft bombardier in his "office." Note .50 caliber machine gun swung out of the way to the right. The ammunition track is empty, indicating a mission other than combative.* Ernest R. McDowell

One of the weird aerial concoctions of World War II was the Messerschmitt Me 163, a tiny rocket-powered interceptor. It was the fastest aircraft in the world at that time. Designed and built in the final days of the Third Reich to combat the growing fleets of Allied bombers, the strange craft had a brief, accident-studded career. It killed more pilots per flying hour than any other aircraft, mainly from the effects of the highly corrosive fuel employed. Picture shows one of these strange craft taking off. Plane used a jettisonable dolly that dropped off when the rocket plane became airborne. It landed on a skid power off, and its total fuel supply at full power lasted slightly over eleven minutes. John Campbell

A Bf 110 that ran afoul of a Spitfire during the Battle of Britain. Downed Me 110s and Junkers Ju 87s littered the English landscape in the late months of 1940. John Campbell

were sending back alarming reports of their inadequacies.

Help was on the way. Brand new P-51s (originally developed and built for the British) were arriving in increasing numbers in late 1943. The Mustang was a long-range fighter *par excellence* and, with the introduction of the large disposable drop tanks, they were able to accompany the bomber streams to the farthest extent of the German nation. The new tanks also improved the escort range of the P-47 and it, too, played a major part in the successes enjoyed by the Eighth during the remainder of the war. The P-38, with its inadequate cockpit heating system, did not fare well at extreme altitude and was not an effective long-range escort fighter. We still had losses, of course, and gunners continued to believe they were doing better than official records indicated.

German fighter pilot losses mounted in direct proportion to our fighter escort increases, not because the *Jagdflieger* exhibited any loss of enthusiasm or morale, but because they were vulnerable to the escorting fighters while attacking the bomber streams! Some of the highest-scoring German aces were killed, although many, with extraordinary flying skill, made it through the war and took their places in the postwar German Air Force. The *Jagdwaffe* was overwhelmed, but if the Luftwaffe higher echelons, primarily Goering himself, had been receptive to fighter pilot recommendations, they would have utilized the superior Me-262 in its intended role as a jet fighter when it was first available. The air war in Europe would certainly have had far different results if Goering had only listened. The Allies would still have won, of course, but their losses, both bombers and fighters, would have been much higher. The salient lesson learned, in addition to the necessity for escorted missions, was that if gunners were to be effective at all, they needed training more realistic than that provided by firing .30 caliber machine guns at towed targets and shotguns on skeet ranges.

The Luftwaffe's *Experten*

The major problem facing gunners in the European air war was the quality of the opposition. According to many recognized aviation historians, the German *Jagdwaffe* could very well have been the finest group of fighter pilots ever assembled. It cannot be compared to any other force in the world, and its toll of destruction was immense. The record these *jagdflieger* compiled is truly mind boggling: about 70,000 aerial victories with another 25,000 aircraft destroyed on the ground. These figures are confirmed with as accurate a system as that employed by the Americans or British. The exceptional period of intense warfare these men were subjected to had a great bearing on these figures, but skill and all-around competence were also involved. Imagine, 4,750 American B-17s were lost during World War II, and of this number the largest percentage succumbed to the guns of the *Jagdwaffe*. Anti-aircraft fire, accidents and the Japanese accounted for some, but German fighter pilots were our most fearful adversaries.

Until faced with overwhelming numerical superiority, the Germans more than held their own. Ask any bomber gunner and he'll attest to the ferocious and determined attacks of the *Jagdflieger*. Much like the RAF in 1940, they were fighting to protect their homeland, undoubtedly a strong motivating factor in both instances.

I had the opportunity to meet, talk and even fly with some of the well-known German fighter aces when I was stationed in Germany from 1955 through 1957. At that time I was assigned to the newly activated 7330th Flying Training Wing, formed for the purpose of training the new West German Air Force. Germany had been occupied for ten years and was finally granted autonomy in May of 1955.

Wing headquarters was located at Fuerstenfeldbruck Air Base, originally one of the Nazis' fine flying facilities. Built in the late thirties to the specifications of Reichsmarshall Hermann Goering, it was designed to compete with or surpass our own Randolph Air Force Base, long considered the foremost flying training installation in the world. This German air base derived its name from the nearby lovely Bavarian village of the same name, some fifteen miles west of Munich.

With few exceptions, American personnel stationed at "Fursty" for the 2½ years it took to construct the modern Luftwaffe in our image (some maintain we did them no favor) professed delight with their assignments. I fondly remember the rustic countryside and quaint villages, the nearby alpine resorts and the beautiful airfield whose buildings were constructed of native stone in typical German architectural style.

But what I remember most are the many former Luftwaffe fighter aces who appeared in our training complex, such well-known *Experten* (the German term for "aces") as: Erich Hartmann with an astounding 352 kills, a record which will never be duplicated; Walter Krupinski, 197 victories; Johannes Steinhoff, 176; and Dietrich Hrabak (the first German wing commander at Fuerstenfeldbruck), who downed 125 aircraft in combat.

All of these men entered the new Luftwaffe as soon as West Germany was granted sovereignty. They started at Landsberg flying our simple T-6 (actually the Canadian Harvard, in most respects identical to our venerable trainer) and graduated to the T-33 jet trainer at Fuerstenfeldbruck. As assistant and later director of the pilot training group's academic department, I saw them all as they came up from Landsberg. I talked with them on many occasions and I also conducted some of their classes. I came to know them well.

Because English had become the ICAO (International Civil Aviation Organization) language of the air, all of the classes at Fuerstenfeldbruck were given in English. Some thirteen German instructors were em-

Ground school was an important part of training the new German Air Force. Here the author conducts an engineering class using mockup of J-33 jet engine. The three German students were young, inexperienced fighter pilots when World War II ended. They were apt pupils and became proficient jet pilots. Author's collection

Some of the instructors and students in front of the Pilot Training Group's academic department. Shown with author (suntan, uniform near center) are seven German instructors and six foreign students. Prior to beginning German instruction, the Flying Training Wing trained a large number of MDAP (Mutual Defense Assistance Pact) nations' fighter pilots. Author's collection

ployed in our department, and after I was named director, Major Joachim Vogt became my German counterpart.

One morning he came into our office and said, "Captain, do you know that we have Germany's top World War II ace in a class this morning?" I didn't; at that time I had no idea who Germany's top ace might be. So, during the first class break, Vogt directed me to Captain Erich Hartmann and introduced me.

I had only a little time to visit but my interest was aroused. In subsequent meetings I learned that he had earned all of his victories on the Eastern Front, mostly against Russians, although five of his kills were against American pilots flying Mustangs in Hungary toward the end of the war. He was captured and turned over to the Russians who incarcerated him for ten years. He was harshly mistreated, as were all of the German pilots unfortunate enough to fall into the hands of the Soviets; some of them were summarily executed. As most of us now know, the Russians paid scant attention to provisions of the Geneva Convention. One of the black marks chalked up against the Americans is the alacrity with which we turned many prisoners of war over to the Communists. Released in 1955, Hartmann returned immediately to the German Air Force as captain, the rank he held at the end of hostilities.

Many of the American instructor pilots flew with Hartmann, mostly out of curiosity. Without exception, American instructors found him to be exceptionally competent at the controls of a T-33, a jet aircraft with which he had very little experience. I could readily understand how this youngster (the Russians referred to him as the "Black Devil") managed his incredible score. He told us he accomplished his feats by approaching as

Erich Hartmann with General Pflugbeil. Note Hartmann's battered cap. German fighter pilots, like their American counterparts, considered the "crusher" a mark of distinction. John Campbell

near his adversary as possible from the rear, and blasting the enemy with one short burst. Hartmann preferred machine guns to the cannon, but even with these lesser weapons, he consistently blew the opposing aircraft apart so completely that flying debris posed a real hazard. He was downed a number of times, mostly from flying aircraft parts. Deflection shooting, he insisted, was used rarely and only on those occasions when a better position could not be obtained. He flew the Messerschmitt Bf 109, a much superior aircraft to the ones he usually encountered. His Knight's Cross with Oak Leaves, Swords and Diamonds, the highest award given to German fighting men during World War II, was indeed beautiful, completely unlike any decoration any of us had ever seen.

(The Knight's Cross with Oak Leaves, Swords and Diamonds, *Ritterkreuz mit Eichenlaub, Schwerter und Brillanten,* was awarded to only twelve individuals during World War II and only by Hitler himself. The award was a continuation of the standard Iron Cross, which had been an esteemed award of the German military since 1813. There were two higher awards, the Golden Oak Leaves and the Grand Cross, special medals given only to Reichsmarshall Hermann Goering.)

I noticed Johannes Steinhoff one day in the hallway

Johannes Steinhoff, one of the Luftwaffe's foremost fighter pilots, had 176 kills when he was seriously injured taking off in an Me 262 jet during the final days of World War II. Steinhoff returned to the new West German Luftwaffe and became chief of staff with the rank of four-star general. Author's collection

of our academic department building. My attention was drawn to him by his horribly burned face and I asked Major Vogt about him. I learned that he was one of Germany's top *Experten* with 176 aerial victories. He, along with Adolph Galland and a few of the other well-known aces, confronted Hermann Goering in the well-documented "Fighter Mutiny" in January of 1945. He was the recipient of the Knight's Cross with Oak Leaves and Swords.

He suffered burns on April 8, 1945, when his Messerschmitt Me 262, the famous German jet fighter in which he finished the war, experienced a takeoff mishap at Munich and smashed into the ground at 125 mph. This was to have been his 900th mission. Steinhoff, "Macki" to his friends, fought his way out of his burning aircraft and survived to become a four-star general and Luftwaffe chief of staff in the seventies.

Steinhoff's daughter Ursula is married to Mike Bird, a Colorado state senator. They reside in Colorado Springs where the general also owns a home. Steinhoff visits the United States on a regular basis and usually spends part of the summer in Colorado Springs.

Steinhoff is an author of some note, having written three books and coauthored another. The last, with Drs. Pechel and Showalter, was just recently released. One of his works, *Wohin treibt die NATO? (Whither NATO?)* is available only in Germany and Japan.

Walter Krupinski was one of the famous *Experten* who gained fame and respect as a foremost tactics teacher. He was the swashbuckling type, a fearless pilot who never lost a wingman in 1,100 combat missions. He helped and protected many beginners and managed to score 197 victories in the process. He was transferred from the Russian front back to Germany in the spring of 1944 to help combat the US bombings. He was particularly proficient in this capacity, especially after he joined the jet fighter unit in March of 1945. I remember him as a "character," a raconteur who was always ready with a quip.

Dietrich Hrabak, who reentered the Luftwaffe as a full colonel, became well-known to all of us at Fuerstenfeldbruck. As German wing commander he served opposite his US counterpart, our own Colonel Mark Vinzant. Hrabak's career differed a bit from other *Jagdflieger.* He enlisted in the German navy in 1934 and transferred to the Luftwaffe two years later.

Dieter was no natural pilot, having cracked up a number of planes during flying training. In 1938 he was posted to Austria and in one year became his unit's *Gruppenkommandeur* (group commander). At the beginning of the Polish campaign, he was one of the very first *Jagdflieger* to be shot down. He scored his first victory on May 13, 1940, during the French campaign and from there, his score mounted. He fought in the Battle of Britain and later served in the Balkans and in Russia commanding various units. He earned the Knight's Cross with Oak Leaves and shot down 125 enemy aircraft. He was one of the first to travel to the US for jet fighter training, and he, together with Steinhoff and others, worked with then Chancellor Adenauer in forming the new West German air force. He was well liked by the American personnel, most of whom knew him well.

These are just a few of the famous World War II Luftwaffe pilots who did so much damage to our bombers in the European theater. In addition, there was Adolf Galland, one of the earliest and best known of the German fighter pilots who, because of his high rank in the German air force, was not permitted to rejoin when Germany was granted sovereignty. I met him on one of his visits to Fuerstenfeldbruck and conversed with him. I had read his book, *Die Ersten und die Letzte (The First and the Last)*, a most impressive work.

Descendant of a Huguenot family that emigrated to Germany from France many years ago (this accounts for his non-Germanic surname), Galland began flying training at nineteen and graduated to powered aircraft in 1932. He was promoted to *Oberleutnant* (equivalent to our first lieutenant) in 1937 and shortly thereafter went to Spain with the Condor Legion. There he flew the antiquated Heinkel He-51 biplanes and scored no victories.

When World War II broke out in 1939, Galland began the phenomenal rise in rank and influence that the Allies remember. He was particularly successful in the Battle of Britain, and subsequent to the accidental death of Werner Moelders, was catapulted to the position of general of the fighter arm late in 1941, the youngest general in the German armed forces. Having won the Knights Cross with Oak Leaves and Swords early in his career, he was awarded the Diamonds on January 28, 1942, the second German to receive the brillanten.

Stories abound of Galland's penchant for cigars. He was a constant smoker, consuming up to twenty cigars a day. He even wrote an order giving himself permission to smoke while on missions! His Messerschmitt was the only fighter in existence with a cigar lighter and he had a holder installed in which he placed his cigar while he was on oxygen.

Galland was constantly at odds with Herman Goering who always blamed the *Jagdwaffe* for the results of the imbecilic decisions his office produced. Galland was finally relieved from his lofty position after the fighter pilot mutiny; subsequently he was appointed to form and head up a squadron of jet fighters. This

Adolf Galland was the youngest general officer in the Luftwaffe when he was appointed head of the fighters. Note the Knight's Cross at his throat. Walter A. Musciano

Adolf Galland departing his Bf 109 after a combat mission. Note the ever-present cigar. Galland smoked the stogies constantly, as many as twenty a day. He had a cigar lighter installed in his airplane. German flying boots were the finest worn by any pilot in World War II. Soft, warm and comfortable, they were prized above all else by American flight crews. When a German crewman was captured, the first thing to go was his boots. John Campbell

The first jet fighter was the Messerschmitt Bf 262, shown here with American markings after its capture. The 262 was a fearful adversary, far faster than anything the Allies could put in the air. Hitler's stubborn insistence on using the aircraft as a bomber was an error of the first magnitude. It entered combat late in the war, after the outcome had already been decided, but it caused consternation among the Allied brass. It was flown by some of the top German aces, including Galland and Steinhoff. John Campbell

renowned JV 44 (*Jaegerverband 44*) contained some of the finest fighter pilots in the world. Galland scored his 104th and final victory, a US B-26, on April 24, 1945.

There were other fine German fighter pilots, many of whom registered exceptionally high scores in combat. Gerhard Barkhorn was a close competitor to Hartmann on the Eastern Front and wound up with 301 confirmed kills. Otto Kittel had 267 victories and Theodor Weissenberger downed 208 opponents. Aviation historians will recognize the name of Werner Moelders who, prior to his death in November of 1941, had registered 115 confirmed victories. If he had lived, even occupying the exalted position of general of the fighters which would have restricted his combat activity, he probably would have been close to the top among German fighter pilots. Walter Nowotny, killed flying the Me 262 jet fighter on November 8, 1944, was the fifth-ranked *Experten* with 258 victories. And then there was Hans-Joachim Marseille, a legend at twenty-two, a free spirit who became the highest scorer against the RAF in North Africa in just one year. He flew 388 sorties and downed 157 aircraft, all British. He was reputedly the finest marksman in the German Air Force, gaining a number of kills with difficult deflection shots. He was another *Jagdflieger* who won the Knight's Cross with Oak Leaves, Swords and Diamonds.

The Bf 109 (Me 109) was a formidable fighting craft. It was small but carried a powerful Daimler-Benz inverted V-12 engine that powered all eight models, with the "G" rated at 1475 hp. This last model, the so-called "Gustav," entered service in May 1942. Designed for high altitude interception of Allied daylight bombers, it carried a 20 mm engine cannon firing through the propeller hub, two synchronized 13 mm machine guns in the cowl, and two more 20 mm guns mounted in pods beneath the wings. One later model, the K4, practically identical to the Gustav, was developed late in 1944 and was supplied to very few units. Ernest R. McDowell

It's interesting to note that all of the top German aces chose and flew the Messerschmitt Bf 109, in preference to the Focke Wulf FW 190. Barkhorn, who commanded an FW 190 unit late in the war, flew a 109 (as did his wingman), leading his 190s in combat. The first of the modern German fighters to enter service, over 35,000 109s were produced, and many wound up after the war as first line aircraft of foreign nations. Ironically, the Israeli air force used the Bf 109 against Egyptian Spitfires in the 1948 Israeli-Arab war. In all its variants, up to and including the Bf 109G, the little aircraft more than held its own against the best the Allies could produce. Records show that 615 *Experten* (those with five or more victories) flew the Bf 109, a remarkable record.

We who served and flew with German fighter pilots in the fifties respected and admired them. They were fine hosts. They even asked for and obtained permission to honor our wing commander, Colonel Vinzant, with the *Zapfenstreich* (translated as tattoo, or retreat

The Focke-Wulf FW 190 was a fine fighter with a BMW air-cooled radial engine that in later versions exceeded 2000 hp. The FW 190 was heavily armed and, with its wide landing gear was much easier to land than the Bf 109. It was popular with low-time pilots but the older, more experienced Jagdflieger *preferred the Bf 109.* Ernest R. McDowell

The clean lines of the FW 190 are apparent in this view. Note that the tail wheel is partly retracted and the wide landing gear folds inward. A fine fighter, its performance at altitude was overshadowed by its companion, the Messerschmitt Bf 109. John Campbell

to quarters) ceremony, an unheard of departure from custom. We learned that this symbol of Prussian militarism had been used in the past to recognize retirement for German field marshals. No one less than that rank had ever been so honored and we Americans were the first foreigners to witness the ceremony. Outlawed following World War I when resistance to militarism, typified by the Prussian Junkers, was at its highest, permission for one last performance of the *Zapfenstreich* had to be obtained from the Bonn government. Many of us noticed and commented on the obvious increase in the number of German troops drilling around the base, but none of us was aware of the treat in store until we received our invitations.

We were treated to a fine dinner at the officers' club that evening, and about nine o'clock General Kammhuber, then commanding general of the West German Luftwaffe, invited us all outside to the front of the building. When we assembled, with Kammhuber, Col. Vinzant and Col. Hrabak in front, we could hear the strains of martial music coming from the distance. In another few minutes we saw entering the base through the main gate approximately two blocks away a marching phalanx of men. I would estimate that there were about 200 in the group, consisting of torch bearers in front and back, with a band and arms-bearing troops in the center.

The formation marched down the base main street parallel to the thoroughfare on which the club was located, then came back on our street and halted in front of the viewing group. They faced us, torches still flaming and band playing, and after a period of time the troops with rifles performed an impressive manual of arms, the likes of which none of the Americans had ever witnessed. Families from the nearby military housing area had gathered alongside the street and were able to view the proceedings.

The entire ceremony lasted about thirty minutes and it was very impressive. Not a sound came from the spectators and after the group had departed, the military dependents slowly and silently made their way home while we returned to the club. We were all visibly moved, especially our base commander.

We were subsequently informed that this was probably the last time the *Zapfenstreich* would ever be performed. It was an occasion I'll never forget.

As a final gesture, General Kammhuber surprised all of the American pilots serving at Fuerstenfeldbruck at an officers' "Dining In" toward the end of our tour; he presented each of us with a pair of the old Luftwaffe wings, the wreath enclosing an eagle clutching a swastika. Since the hated swastika emblem had been banned in postwar Germany, we were told that the decorations had been manufactured in Switzerland and smuggled into Germany. Enclosed in a beautiful red leather box and lying on red velvet, the wings were presented by the general himself, accompanied by a hearty handshake. I shall always treasure this bit of memorabilia.

Herrn

Capt. Ivan L. H i c k ma n

Fürstenfeldbruck, Air Base

Sehr geehrter Herr Hauptmann !

Der Kommandeur des Kommandos der Schulen gibt sich zugleich im Namen des Inspekteurs der Luftwaffe die Ehre, Sie zu der am 29. Juni 1957 um 11 Uhr im Kinosaal stattfindenden Abschiedsfeier für

COL. MARK H. VINZANT JR.

und zum Abendessen um 19 Uhr mit anschließendem Beisammensein und Zapfenstreich ergebenst einzuladen.

Der Ständige Vertreter des Kommandeurs

(ENNECCERUS)
Oberstleutnant

The author's formal invitation to a special ceremony honoring the American wing commander, Col. Mark H. Vinzant, Jr. The Zapfenstreich was an old Prussian military rite given only at the retirement of a German field marshal. It had been outlawed since the end of World War I and the Bonn government gave special permission for this final honor. Author's collection

Author reestablished contact with a German acquaintance after returning to the United States. Photo, taken in 1962 at Headquarters Ninth Aerospace Defense Division in Colorado Springs, shows author with Capt. Judel, at that time a language instructor at the US Air Force Academy. Dr. Judel is admiring author's Luftwaffe pilot wings, presented by General Kammhuber at Fuerstenfeldbruck, Germany in 1957. Author's collection

As it was in the beginning 2

Today it seems strange that belligerent nations of World War I could not at first fully appreciate the airplane as a weapon of war. There were the dreamers, of course, but hidebound military traditionalists just couldn't bring themselves to understand the potential of this new gadget.

Experimentations abounded, to be sure. Not long after the Wright brothers brought forth this modern marvel, the United States purchased an "aeroplane" and the Signal Corps began testing it, intending it for use strictly in a reconnaissance and communications capacity. "Chairborne" military bigwigs envisioned this new tool as a spy in the sky, a mobile form of Thaddeus Lowe's Civil War balloons. To hang bombs or machine guns on the flimsy airframes of the day committed unthinkable heresy to the simplistic minds of that time.

Many airwar proponents attempted to convert the traditionalists. As early as 1912, a US Army captain named Charles **DeF.** Chandler went aloft in a Wright Model B biplane (the pilot was Lt. Roy T. Kirkland) cradling a .30 caliber Lewis machine gun between his legs. At an altitude of perhaps 300 feet—the exact height is unknown because there were no sensitive altimeters in those days—Chandler fired a drum of forty-seven rounds at a canvas sheet on the ground and registered six hits. This was significantly impressive in light of latter-day gunnery scores.

Shortly thereafter other tests were conducted, mostly by English and French marksmen. They obtained similar results using the Lewis, the machine gun destined to become the preeminent aerial weapon among the Allied powers after the airplane was accepted as a legitimate military machine. The Lewis would remain in wide use by many nations for the next thirty years.

The Lewis had a long, prestigious life. A fine machine gun, it experienced a minimum of changes and modifications over the years. Well into the thirties it retained most of the superior mechanical characteristics that created its popularity in the beginning. (Originally it weighed some 26½ pounds and fired at the rate of 560 rounds per minute.) Later, engineers improved its rate of fire slightly and reduced its weight by eliminating the air-cooling jacket, relying on the airstream aloft for cooling. The former cumbersome installation was thus replaced by a much easier-to-operate weapon.

The Germans did not stand idly by. When war broke out in 1914, they possessed machine guns superior in many respects to those employed by England and France. Their drum-fed Parabellum 7.92 mm air-cooled machine gun was superior, in some respects, to the Lewis. Its unmatched 700 rounds per minute rate of fire helped considerably in overcoming the lighter Allied weapon, even though the Lewis was usually mounted in pairs.

The Allies and Central Powers employed fine, belt-fed machine guns on fixed mounts to fire through the propeller arc on aircraft used as fighters later in the conflict. The Germans had the 7.92 mm Spandau, and the English and French used the Vickers. Both fine weapons, generally trouble free and of approximately the same caliber, were used throughout World War I.

England, Belgium, France, Italy and Russia all experimented in varying degrees with airborne armament after proving aerial combat feasible. All apparently recognized the inevitability of hostilities during the early years of the twentieth century, and it is difficult to understand why months passed after the outbreak of the first great conflict before aircraft crews began to fire at each other with the express intent of

Captain Chandler (left) with pilot Lieutenant Kirtland in early Wright biplane prior to flight in which first airborne firing occurred in 1912. On this auspicious occasion Capt. Chandler fired a drum of forty-seven rounds at a canvas target on the ground and scored six hits. Note Lewis machine gun with original air-cooling jacket. On later models, the heavy jacket was discarded, relying on airstream to keep barrel cool. US Air Force

Capt. Chandler firing Lewis machine gun on ground range. Photo gives clear view of early cumbersome weapon. Note ammunition drum on top between weapon sights. Drum held forty-seven rounds. This configuration lasted until the Lewis was replaced by the Browning .30 caliber in the thirties. US Air Force

inflicting harm. Stories abound of early clumsy attempts by pilots and observers to engage in aerial combat with pistols and rifles.

Airplanes of the early 1900s were extremely fragile in comparison to today's sophisticated machines. Equipped with undependable internal combustion engines, they could barely lift a single passenger to a worthwhile altitude, and any additional weight severely penalized them in performance. One notable exception was the British Vickers No. 18 "Destroyer," originally contracted by the admiralty as early as 1912. Conceived as a "fighting aeroplane" with a mounted machine gun,

Gun cameras were used for flexible gunnery training as long ago as the early twenties. In this crude adaptation, what appears to be simple box camera may be seen just ahead of gunner's right hand. Note absence of ammunition drum and the standard Scarff mounting. US Air Force

it was envisioned obviously as an offensive craft. Someone other than a military traditionalist must have had a hand in this exception to the prevalent beliefs of the time. Designed with a pusher engine to permit a gun to be mounted in a forward nacelle, Vickers thus eliminated the problem of firing through the propeller arc. (Remember, this was 1912.) The plane saw no action. However, it served as the predecessor of the similar FB-5 "Gun Bus," which performed creditably on the Western Front during the first two years of combat.

Aerial warfare accelerated aircraft design and tactics wondrously during World War I and while armament kept pace, training of aerial gunners consisted mostly of trial and error. Many factors inhibited the flexible gun's accuracy. (The term "flexible" distinguished it from the fixed gun.) Attached to a mount, the flexible machine gun could be moved and aimed up, down, right and left. While pilots of single-seat fighters—known as pursuit aircraft in those days—equipped only with fixed guns firing forward had to aim their planes, multi-seat airplanes with movable mounts enabled gunners to fire at objects in any direction, inhibited only by their own crafts' structures.

The mechanics of aiming a flexible gun proved much more complex than those affecting the fixed weapon. While the pilot with a fixed gun always fired at targets in the same plane as his aircraft, the operator of a flexible gun had to contend with various angles and levels. Those who have fired machine guns in both modes (many of the World War I fighter aces began their military careers as observers in two-seaters), insist that aiming an aircraft carrying fixed weapons is much the simpler of the two. Developed only in later years, sophisticated computing sights were intended to assist the gunner in this unenviable and ofttimes frustrating task. Aerial gunnery most certainly is one of the more inexact sciences. Since the advent of aerial warfare, aircraft gunners have expended millions of rounds of ammunition from both fixed and flexible guns without effect.

Although the tractor-type airplane (with the propeller in front) flew faster than the pushers, they suffered serious disadvantages during the early stages of the war. At first no one knew how to mount a machine gun to fire forward without damaging the whirling blades of a tractor airplane. On the other hand, with engine and propeller in the rear, pushers adapted admirably to aerial warfare. Located in the nose of the aircraft, the gunner had an unobstructed field of fire forward, the only area of concern at that time.

Even before the war, experiments carried out in France led indirectly to the first aerial combat. A tremendously heavy piece of ordnance for a 1913 vintage aircraft, a 37 mm cannon was fitted to and successfully fired from a crude Voisin biplane. As early as October 5, 1914 (remember, World War I began in August of that year), two Frenchmen, Sergeant Joseph Frantz and his mechanic/gunner, Corporal Louis Quenault, were cruising behind the German lines in their Voisin pusher biplane on a mission to bomb enemy concentrations, a rare event for this stage of combat. Suggested by foresighted Gabriel Voisin, designer and builder of this airplane and fourteen others of No. 24 Squadron, this aircraft had recently been armed with an 8 mm Hotchkiss machine gun. The famed French designer had even come up with a special tubular mounting, placing the weapon above the pilot's head. Seated behind the pilot (both cockpits were located ahead of the wings), the gunner had an unrestricted field of fire, both ahead and to the sides. The upper wing restricted the gunner's vision to the rear but this mattered little. The Germans only had reconnaissance airplanes at that time, mostly unarmed (except for an occasional handgun) and, because they were tractor types, crews could not fire directly ahead.

Shortly after crossing the lines, Sgt. Frantz spotted a German Aviatik biplane slightly below and east of his position. The German carried a rifle but could fire only to the sides and rear. Frantz tried to maneuver the German craft over the French lines, and after a series of dives and banks with each pilot trying to outmaneuver the other, the Frenchman finally prevailed. Over Allied territory at an altitude of some 600 feet, gunners in both airplanes fired at each other intermittently with no damage to show for their efforts.

It should be noted that Quenault, even with a machine gun, did not possess the advantage a person

Double Lewis machine gun mounting on post-World War One Army observation aircraft. Note absence of former air-cooling jacket and the Scarff mount. The Lewis was a light weapon and double (and even triple) installations were common during the twenties. US Air Force

might think. Not at all the reliable weapon it would later become, the Hotchkiss was plagued with an awkward feed system that had to be cleaned and adjusted after about twenty-five rounds. As a result, Quenault was only firing single shots and after some forty rounds, the gun jammed. The Frenchman frantically worked to clear his weapon, but during the interval the German plane went out of control and crashed. Quenault's last shot had killed the opposing pilot Wilhelm Schlichting who, with his observer Fritz von Zangen, became the first airmen to die in combat.

The knowledge derived from this first aircraft duel took some time to penetrate the unimaginative minds of the military theorists of the day, but in mid-1915 the French abandoned the few archaic Hotchkiss machine guns and the ubiquitous cavalry carbines, and replaced them with the lighter, simpler and more effective Lewis. The Germans at this time did not have a suitable flexible gun, relying on the cavalry carbine until development of the excellent Parabellum. As a matter of fact, neither side totally abandoned the rifle, even after the machine gun had come into general use in the air. Indeed, the rifle did remarkably well in the hands of trained marksmen, and a number of kills were made with the weapon.

As late as July 25, 1915, Captain Lanoe G. Hawker in a Bristol Scout shot down two German two-seaters and forced another to land, armed only with a single-shot carbine. Mounted on the starboard side of the single-seat fighter's fuselage, the weapon pointed obliquely to the right to avoid the propeller arc, an interesting arrangement soon widely copied. In recognition of his feat, Hawker won the Victoria Cross and became the first of many British air heroes to receive England's highest military decoration.

The machine gun finally came into general use, although in light of later developments, with extremely crude mountings. For tractor fighters, the weapons were mostly mounted on the aircraft fuselage sides like Hawker's rifle. The two-seaters, mainly pushers, flew considerably slower. Only later did tractor two-seaters with the gunner seated behind the pilot come into general use. Innovations with single-seat fighters came swiftly, however, and with them combat in the air became a deadly science.

Early in the fighter experimentation phase, someone mounted a machine gun on the upper wing, designed to fire forward. This permitted the pilot for the first time to aim his aircraft directly (although somewhat nose down) at a target. When a sliding rail

The German Parabellum mounted on a World War I Rumpler two-seater. With the fastest rate of fire of any machine gun used during the First World War, the Parabellum was a fine weapon. It, like the Lewis, was drum fed but, unlike the Lewis, the drum was mounted vertically. The German mount was inferior to the Scarff which was used by all the Allies. Smithsonian Institution

system was devised so the pilot could pull his weapon down to change the ammunition drum (the Lewis was the only gun used in this fashion), pusher aircraft were doomed.

It remained for a French pilot to point the way for forward firing through the propeller arc. Ronald Garros had made a name for himself before the war by flying across the Mediterranean Sea and winning a number of prewar air races. Copying a leaf from the experiments conducted by Raymond Saulnier, Garros fitted steel wedge-shaped deflector plates to the propeller blades of his Morane-Saulnier monoplane in such a manner that a machine gun could be mounted on the fuselage ahead of him and aimed to fire safely through the propeller arc. Some of the bullets were kicked aside by the steel blades, but the majority of them went through. It was an effective development that completely revolutionized aerial combat.

Garros made his device work because he didn't wait for approval from higher headquarters. On April 1, 1915, prior to Hawker's success with a carbine, he shot down a German aircraft and followed that with another five within the next two weeks. News of this terrible new weapon was not long in reaching the Germans, of course, and when Garros suffered engine failure and was forced down behind enemy lines (he had been directed to avoid German territory; his disobedience cost the Allies dearly), the secret was out. (It's interesting to note that Saulnier had even developed a synchronizing gear by mechanically linking the machine gun trigger to a cam on the engine crankshaft so the weapon's fire would be synchronized to avoid the propeller blades. However, in ensuing tests the still unreliable Hotchkiss tended to "hang fire," endangering the wooden blades. Saulnier then fitted steel plates to the blades but the French War Department wasn't interested and the idea died a-borning. Actually, synchronization wasn't all that new. A Russian designer, Lieutenant Poplavko and a German, Franz Schneider, in addition to the Edwards brothers in Great Britain, had come up with similar devices before the war but couldn't sell their ideas to their respective military chiefs.)

It was not long before the brilliant Dutchman Anthony Fokker designed and installed a practical synchronization gear on his new Eindekker airplane. With this development, aerial combat suddenly assumed a remarkable level of efficiency and established a form that would prevail for generations.

Thus, out of necessity, the tractor two-seater was born and with it a host of problems never before envisaged. The English pushers proved especially vulnerable to the swift, forward-firing single-seat fighters, and the scramble was on to develop two-seaters with the gunner seated behind the pilot and firing to the rear, the area from which almost all attacks came.

The first tentative experiments had borne fruit and individual aerial entrepreneurs came up with many ideas, some practical, others not. Said to be the brain child of a pilot caught over the lines with no accompanying protection, formation flying soon came to the fore. After learning that success depended on numbers, the French and British adopted formation flying and initiated flights of three or four airplanes strictly for defensive purposes. Soon the Germans' swarms, the dreaded "Flying Circuses," followed, developed to a devastating degree by a number of brilliant German aces. The best known, the famous Baron von Richthofen, wound up as the war's leading ace with eighty victories, all made during the incredibly short period of 1½ years. His first kill came on September 17, 1916 and he died in combat April 21, 1918.

The success of the Germans' new tactics brought additional developments on the Allied side. Concentrating now on faster two-seaters, the British and French settled on the Lewis gun mounted on an ingenious ring invented by and named after an Englishman, Warrant Officer F. W. Scarff, to provide protection to the rear. The Germans kept pace with their Parabellum, although their gun mount was not as good as the Scarff which remained in widespread use well into the thirties.

The air war really heated up in 1916, with each side developing in turn superior aircraft and tactics. With the advent of the German synchronization gear, the Allies relied on a stopgap measure, the upper wing-mounted Lewis. When synchronization became available to the British and French, they selected the Vickers as the universal forward-firing gun. The upper-mounted Lewis had its proponents, however, and the SE-5, arguably the finest single-seat fighter of the war, continued to mount the Lewis right up to the end of the war. Many British aces achieved their exalted status using the Lewis.

Air-minded officers, decidedly in the minority during World War I, knew early in the conflict that aircraft could and should play a larger combat role than previously envisioned. They pressed for other uses, convinced that bombs could be delivered by air with a telling effect. Before bombing became an integral part of aerial warfare, various adventuresome pilots had experimented with dropping hand grenades on enemy troops and installations, and while results were at best minimal, it soon became obvious this newly devised tactic held promise. It was not long before bombs, as we know them today, were developed. Originally carried in the rear cockpit, they became the responsibility of the overtaxed observer to drop them. No aiming device existed in 1916 of course, and the observer heaved the bombs over the side whenever he judged himself in position to hit his designated target.

This clumsy, inaccurate system begged for improvement, and by the end of the war, large specialized aircraft came into general use, equipped with bomb racks and bomb release mechanisms and heavily protected by numerous flexible machine guns. These were positioned so that few blind spots were left for marauding fighters to take advantage of. Originally the bombers flew singly, depending on stealth and surprise to accomplish their missions, but subsequent events dictated other tactics. By 1917, bombers flew in formation, escorted and protected by fighter screens. Introducing this new concept, the Germans employed sufficient numbers of bombers to be effective, and swept the skies of enemy aircraft by an overwhelming number of protective fighters. The lessons learned were unfortunately lost with the passage of time and with near-disastrous results, as discovered in a later conflict.

We now know that stringent measures should have been taken in the very beginning to properly train embryo gunners, but to the military thinkers of World War I, aircraft needed a mapreader in preference to a gunner. Gunnery training for observers was practically nonexistent until early in 1916, and after that it became more a hit-or-miss proposition than a formal and systematized program. As the litmus test of gunners' capabilities, fighter pilots displayed almost utter disdain in their attacks from the rear. Some of them paid for their cavalier attitudes, but they usually considered it a lucky hit whenever an observer downed an opponent. The pilots of two-seaters firing forward made a good many more kills, although the percentage of victories tallied by the slower aircraft was minimal compared to the more agile single-seaters.

Most of the experts in policy-making positions failed to differentiate aerial gunnery from other, more familiar types of gunnery such as hunting for birds or small game. It seemed to them a simple matter: just take an experienced hunter familiar with leads appropriate for a startled game bird, put him in an airplane and he would achieve results similar to a hunting foray in an open field with shotgun at the ready. It didn't work that way. Aerial gunners found themselves faced with the frustrating task of relearning how to aim a weapon using a relatively cumbersome machine gun with an inefficient ring and bead sight, and with entirely different lead and ballistics characteristics from anything in their experience. Deflection allowance, left to the instinctive initiative of the individual, proved less than productive, to say the least.

The United States entered the conflict in 1917 having lagged in preparation for the coming hostilities. The few aircraft available to the Army Signal Corps Aviation Section, forerunner of our modern Air Force, were of such dubious quality that very little thought had been given to arming them. A few feeble attempts to mount a Lewis machine gun on the archaic biplanes we then possessed were largely ineffective. Determined efforts at gunnery training, especially flexible gunnery, were not implemented until many years later.

Great Britain took some preliminary steps and in September of 1915 formed a machine gun school, later to become the No. 1 (Observers) School of Aerial Gunnery. At the same time and in consonance with the still prevalent role of aircraft in reconnaissance and artillery spotting, they instituted a course in wireless telegraphy. Initially, the gunnery school concentrated on ground instruction, but sometime later made an effort to add aerial gunnery training as an important adjunct. In 1916, another British school became operational at Camiers on the French coast, with emphasis on updating current aerial combat techniques. Another school opened in Egypt in 1917, and before the end of hostilities three auxiliary schools were sanctioned in the United Kingdom. In all of these training endeavors, ground school primarily concentrated on weapons nomenclature and repair. The relatively little air training in the course consisted mostly of firing at sleeve targets towed parallel to the gunner's aircraft, training that provided a major part of later gunnery programs—which we now know was of dubious value—up and into World War II.

And so ended a terrible conflict, the first in which this newly developed aerial weapon, which promised so much and delivered so little, was used. There was no doubt in the minds of dedicated aviation experts that the possibilities demonstrated by aircraft would be realized in a future war. Few could foretell, however, just what the future had in store and especially what role the oft-maligned aerial gunner would occupy a scant twenty-one years later.

The first feeble steps 3

The United States took a leaf from the British system of gunnery training during World War I, and after the end of hostilities continued to concentrate on ground instruction. In the twenties and early thirties, this consisted primarily of nomenclature, stripping and assembling weapons, range practice and lectures on sights. The Air Force conducted some aerial instruction both with camera and machine guns using the Norman compensating foresight and the standard ring and bead. Both gauged the respective speeds of the gunner's aircraft and the target, albeit crudely compared to developments a short time later. Concurrent with post-World War I ennui and a massive reduction in our military forces, gunnery training became an extremely low priority function.

What evidence exists regarding the continuity of gunnery training could be found at the Army flying schools, first at Brooks Field, San Antonio, Texas (primary), then transferred in 1925 to the advanced flying school at nearby Kelly Field. Here gunnery training was included in the flying course for cadets and regular Army officers. As late as 1928, however, only one JN-6H airplane, the venerable "Jenny" most readily associated with early barnstorming days, was available there for gunnery. This phase of the flying program lagged far behind.

The first faint glimmer of standardization began to appear in 1927 at Wright Field where specialized ranges, equipped with targets, frames and bulletproof dugouts for observers, were constructed for flexible gunnery training. Shortly thereafter, annual machine gun and bombing matches were initiated Air Force-wide, with one competition specifically allocated to flexible gunners.

Attention to flexible gunnery continued to increase in the 1930s, evidenced by specifications to bidders for construction of the Martin B-10 bomber. Advanced for its day, this aircraft featured the following equipment: two Lewis guns in front and another pair in the rear with Type B flexible gun mounts (a modification of the Scarff) in each gunner's cockpit; twenty Lewis gun magazines; three Lewis gunsights; and two Lewis windvane flexible gunsights. (The last named developments provided the gunner with an indication of his aircraft's speed, thus assisting in estimating lead.) With all this equipment, the defensive capability of an otherwise fine aircraft suffered, however, from the less-than-competent personnel operating the armament.

Machine gun mounts came in for some close scrutiny during this period, occasioned mostly by operational difficulties with the standard Scarff. Aircraft flew faster as the years passed and gunners found it increasingly difficult to manhandle antiquated equipment against the stronger slipstreams encountered. Many experiments were conducted, resulting in the introduction of a new, heavier and larger mount—but easier nonetheless to manipulate. Also at this approximate time, the first crude turrets appeared. They provided complete protection against the slipstream when mounted in front, but were open in back when facing to the rear. To a great extent, this alleviated the gunner's discomfort and operational difficulties caused by wind blast.

Guns, too, experienced a metamorphosis of sorts and resulted in the finest weapon of World War II. Before the end of the 1920s, the single-barrel Browning .30 caliber machine gun replaced the now outmoded twin Lewis. The British copied this fine Browning weap-

Slow and extremely vulnerable, the Keystone B-3A was the standard US bomber during the late twenties and early thirties. Many World War II general officers obtained their first training in this venerable aircraft. Note the Scarff mount in the nose and side-by-side cockpit to the rear. Smithsonian Institution

The Boeing B-9 bomber, advanced for its day (early thirties), displays the monoplane configuration that would prevail from that time forward. It was the first of the heavy military aircraft to employ retractable landing gear. Twin Lewis machine guns were normally mounted on a modified Scarff ring at the open gunner's station in the nose. Smithsonian Institution

on with slightly larger caliber and used it very successfully on both their fighters and bombers in World War II. However, it did not compare in destructive power to the preeminent Browning .50 caliber, developed in the late thirties. The .50 caliber was introduced just in time to contribute significantly to the outcome of the Second World War. No other nation could match this weapon, and it proved superior in many respects to the larger 20 mm cannon used extensively by the Axis powers. A much heavier machine gun than anything previously carried aloft by US aircraft, the .50 caliber necessitated the development of new accessory equipment. It also required extensive strengthening of airplane structures in the vicinity of gun positions.

By the late 1930s, six Air Force schools were located in various parts of the United States, most of which conducted widely different forms of aerial gunnery, both fixed and flexible. With the imminent outbreak of hostilities in Europe, the US government finally initiated steps to modernize and expand the country's armed forces training posture. The Military Appropriations Act of 1939 set in motion machinery which resulted eventually in the proliferation of military airfields, most of which exist today in various stages of disrepair, dotting the landscape from coast to coast.

With the superb B-17 already in production and other fighting craft on the drawing boards, the Air Corps focused increasingly on the training of personnel to man the armaments carried aloft. At that time our military thinkers envisioned immense fleets of super bombers, armed to the teeth with our new .50 caliber machine guns and able, in close formation, to ward off enemy fighters foolish enough to approach within range of the formation's formidable weaponry. Because of this wishful thinking, as we were to learn later, attacking German fighters were able to destroy exorbitant numbers of our unescorted bombers.

In September of 1940, the newly activated Southeast Air Corps Training Center at Maxwell Field, Alabama, was notified of plans for the establishment of two flexible gunnery training schools and was asked for recommendations. Results of long and extensive planning indicated a woeful lack of expertise in the field of flexible gunnery. The proposed curriculum, extending over a five-week period, would consist of orientation, sighting and range estimates, gun repair, aircraft recognition, ground range exercises, preliminary air exercises

The Martin XB-10, first of the truly "modern" bombers in the US inventory. Note front turret, bombardier's viewing window and fully cowled engines. Pilot was still exposed to the elements in open cockpit. Smithsonian Institution

and air range instruction. It soon became obvious that the proposed training regimen left much to be desired, and the United States of necessity availed itself of all the information gained through combat experience by friendly forces then at war. As a result, and at British invitation, a team of officers went to England to study gunnery training programs then in use by our soon-to-be Allies.

The team study and observation resulted in a report submitted in October by Major W. L. Kennedy, attached at that time to the Office of the Chief of the Air Corps (OCAC). The report became something of a landmark. The recommendations were: send officers on a continuing basis to England to obtain firsthand information on training for actual combat, prepared to study changes in current courses of instruction; provide gunner trainees the opportunity to fire extensively at aerial targets; institute synthetic training devices in the curriculum (but not at the expense of actual firing); assign fighter type aircraft to gunnery schools for the purpose of conducting simulated attacks against gunners "firing" camera guns; prepare well-trained instructors as ". . . the backbone of the gunnery schools"; implement the award of a distinctive badge or emblem to be worn on the uniforms of graduate gunners; and commission a percentage of gunners serving in tactical units.

The very first US flexible gunnery school was established at Las Vegas, Nevada, in 1941. This site, together with those that followed, fulfilled certain established requirements which included excellent flying weather and large areas of available uninhabited public wastelands. The advantages of the location, it was believed, would outweigh the obvious moral disadvantages created by the close proximity of the base to this foremost gambling center.

The initial troops to staff and man the new training facility arrived from Brooks Field on June 17, 1941, but no actual firing training occurred before the Japanese attack on Pearl Harbor. By that time, three classes of slightly more than 100 instructors had graduated. On December 9, the chief of the Air Corps ordered aerial training for gunners. By the end of 1941, West Coast Training Center requested approval to enlarge the Las Vegas school to provide an entering class of 320 students each week. Our burgeoning training efforts showed a constantly increasing flow of students. A total of 10,562 enrolled in 1942 at this desert location and eighty-five percent of them graduated.

Harlingen, at the southernmost tip of Texas, became the next flexible gunnery training school. Despite its proximity to the Mexican border which restricted flights to the south, Harlingen boasted mild winters, relatively comfortable summers and excellent railroad service. In addition, the nearby Gulf of Mexico offered unlimited area for aerial gunnery ranges. Personnel began arriving at Harlingen on September 1, 1941, but training activities did not commence prior to Pearl Harbor. The first class graduated in January of 1942.

With Harlingen originally scheduled to handle a constant student load of 600 and with 120 graduating each week, this number proved insufficient to meet the constantly increasing demands of our combat forces. In July of 1942, the student load increased to 940 and to 1,320 the following October. This still did not meet combat requirements and the quota increased again in April of 1943, this time to 1,900 with an attendant increase in course length to six weeks. (Student load and course length increased proportionately at all schools then in operation.) At the same time, the flow of students also increased significantly. In August of 1943, a total of 360 students per week was required to keep up with combat demands; this was increased in November to 475. In 1942 Harlingen graduated 4,953 students, 15,682 in 1943 and 4,009 during the first two months of 1944.

The next school was established at Tyndall Field near Panama City, Florida. Though authorized as early as April 15, 1941, troops did not arrive until December 7 when 2,000 transferred from nearby Eglin Field. Like Harlingen, Tyndall was an especially suitable location on the Gulf of Mexico, providing large overwater expanses for aerial gunnery ranges. By the end of 1941, it was apparent that Tyndall was incapable of handling the volume of traffic envisioned for the rapidly expanding gunnery program, and a sub-base was activated a short distance to the east at Apalachicola on July 10, 1942. Tyndall graduated 8,091 students in 1942 and a whopping 39,452 two years later.

In consonance with Maj. Kennedy's recommendations, the Air Corps established the first school for flexible gunnery instructors at Buckingham Field, Fort Myers, Florida, on July 5, 1942. The first class entered on September 7, and by the end of the year, more than 3,000 instructors had graduated.

One of the earliest Browning .30 caliber installations. Note the ring and bead sight and the venerable Scarff mount. Gunner is warmly dressed for temperatures encountered at altitude. Helmet and goggles are typical of aircrew attire up through World War II. Smithsonian Institution

Meanwhile, the Air Force was considering other training sites. West Coast Training Command began investigating a location near Kingman, Arizona, in 1941. In terms of climatic conditions, transportation facilities and land suitable for air-to-air firing, Kingman offered decided advantages. A shortage of water, however, was a problem not solved until a year later when engineers discovered sources previously believed unavailable. The school was activated August 4, 1942, although training did not begin until the middle of January 1943. Kingman's late start permitted the school to profit from sound experience and avoid many of the earlier training centers' mistakes. Kingman graduated 10,861 student gunners in 1943.

Welcome to Kingman

My initial impression of Kingman, Arizona, and the newly constructed Army Air Field was most depressing. It was late May of 1943 when my wife and I, newlyweds of just one month, drove up from Phoenix.

I was commissioned March 10 of that year at Luke Field and had completed the course of the Central Instructors' School at Randolph Field, near San Antonio, Texas. Some twenty brand-new second lieutenants from Luke made up our group and most of us had been hoping for combat assignments. Our disappointment was tempered by the assurance that instructing for a year would surely sharpen our piloting skills and we could then anticipate a combat tour with a much better chance for survival. Promises, promises!

The Randolph course was interesting and constructive. We became really proficient in the AT-6, and from that notorious rear cockpit, no less. Those who have experienced night landing in the "Texan" from this blind position can appreciate what I'm saying. The stage commanders were constantly exhorting us and threatening that if we didn't do well, we would be shipped to a flexible gunnery school, a fate worse than death, we were told. We were suitably impressed.

We finished the course, most of us with excellent grades. After graduation, it was back to Luke Field where we inherited our first students. I found myself with six Chinese cadets—but that's another story. I beckoned my bride-to-be who hastened to Phoenix where we were married April 29. And then, just one month later, we all (the original twenty) were reassigned. Where? To a flexible gunnery school, of course. Kingman became home to most of us for the next two years. Ah, the vagaries of chance!

Driving southwest down the highway, we first noticed the base straddling Route 66 and the main line of the Santa Fe Railway. We gave the desolate scene a casual glance, noticing the hastily erected buildings of the main installation south of the railroad, and what turned out to be extensive ground gunnery ranges on the right. We continued on another seven miles and we were in Kingman. My, what a sight!

With some 7,000 prewar population, the little city had been inundated with an influx of military personnel probably equaling that number. Housing of any kind was practically nonexistent to the newcomer, with some personnel living in the most primitive housing one can imagine. Kingman was an unincorporated municipality, believe it or not, and wartime rent controls, so prevalent and stringent in most localities, did not apply here. Dwellings, which would be termed hovels in most other locations, were snapped up as soon as they came on the market. Landlords were demanding and getting exorbitant prices.

We drove down main street, the drab continuation of Route 66, past the Beale Hotel where we would spend our first uncomfortable night in Kingman, then north along rough, graveled streets to the edge of town. We noted with distaste the dingy shacks, most of which we learned were occupied by military personnel. We traversed the community from one end to the other, past relatively affluent neighborhoods which still managed to look seedy, through more slum areas, then back to the highway and on out to the airfield.

The air base was nearly as bad. Evidence of hasty construction remained, the buildings typical of the temporary types found on so many wartime installations. Located at the northeast edge of the field, the officers' open mess was drab and skimpy in appointments. Desert sagebrush encroached, growing close to the club. Wing headquarters was located in a single-story edifice, painted white but unattractive, in front of which was a sparse flower bed outlined with white-washed stones. A flagpole stood forlornly between an asphalt street and headquarters driveway, and a four-block-long dusty parade ground lay to the north. The only decent buildings on the base were the flight line hangars and I've seen better. All in all, a most unpromising beginning.

Added to that, the terrible desert heat was just reaching its afternoon apogee and this did little to elevate our spirits. Of course, universal air conditioning was still in the future but during the two years we spent at Kingman, we came to accept the desert climate and even grew to like it. Looking back now in the comfort of a moderate clime, we remember the good things—but the bad vibes remain.

My wife put it best: "Honey, just what did you do to deserve this?" I attempted to make light of the situation, but I'm afraid I wasn't too convincing. We did experience some enjoyable times at this desert outpost. Our first son was born in Kingman, and we made many friends there. We consoled ourselves with the knowledge that Kingman Army Air Field was probably no worse than many other bases then in existence. Most military people of that time can probably relate similar experiences, but I'm willing to wager that very few lived for a summer in a high school building as twelve of us did.

Out strolling one Sunday afternoon, desperate and seeking living accommodations, we came upon this gentleman working in his front yard and we stopped to visit with him. He turned out to be the Kingman High School principal and when we mentioned our needs, he brought our plight to the attention of the school board. As a result, we were invited to move into the high school building until classes resumed in the fall. It was a godsend. Local residents even provided beds and linen for us, and we spent a comfortable summer sleeping in hallways and classrooms and cooking our meals in the home economics room. By the end of August we all managed to find fairly decent living quarters, at least by Kingman standards, and we'll always warmly remember the kindness demonstrated by some very nice people. I hasten to add that Kingman today is a far different community from the one we knew so many years ago. It is now a progressive, attractive city and the hub of various growing enterprises in northwest Arizona.

I signed in for duty at KAAF the day after my arrival and checked out in the AT-6 the same day. Big deal! I had been instructing cadets in that airplane and, surprisingly, right after my checkout I also flew my first gunnery mission . . . with a frightened student gunner ensconced in the rear seat.

And my wife? Well, she spent the first of many long, lonely days at the Stonywold Motel, awaiting the return of a spouse seemingly spending more time in the air than at home.

Like Kingman and Las Vegas, the next training facility located near Laredo, Texas, boasted fine flying weather and extensive unpopulated areas. Laredo was activated eight days later than Kingman but graduated a class as early as the first week of January 1943. Later it became a prime testing site for advanced flexible gunnery training programs and the final location of the Central Gunnery Instructors School.

The voracious demands for trained gunners continued unabated, and necessity added still another facility. Yuma Army Air Field, at that time an advanced pilot training school, offered climate and wasteland advantages similar to Las Vegas and Kingman and officially became a flexible gunnery training facility November 11, 1943. Gunnery paralleled pilot training there for one month; the latter was then abandoned. Only 113 students graduated in 1943, but by the end of that year, 1,655 were enrolled and undergoing training.

Built hurriedly and usually without time for proper planning, flexible gunnery schools typified many installations constructed to meet wartime exigencies. Remnants of the temporary flying fields dotting our nation's landscape remind many of today's elderly citizens of that time in the early forties when we went to war. Not all of the memories are fond ones. One of the first flexible gunnery instructors in the frantic days of our military build-up, Joseph Koluder remembers the state of near chaos typifying our initial training efforts.

Koluder graduated from armament school at Lowry Field, Denver, Colorado, in September of 1941. From there he was sent to a school squadron at Eglin Field and marked time there until Tyndall, the new base near Panama City, was completed. After months of inactivity, Koluder and his companions were finally transferred.

"It took us three days," he recalls, "to get from Eglin to Panama City on a train that should have been used for firewood instead of transportation. We spent more time on sidings than empty boxcars. To top this all off, we were fed—what else?—field rations! Chili and beef stew the entire trip, a journey that should have been accomplished in two hours."

Koluder's group finally reached Panama City. They pitched their tents on the outskirts of the town because Tyndall was not yet ready for occupancy. Shortly after their arrival, Japan bombed Pearl Harbor and things became interesting right away. Koluder remembers seeing Jimmy Doolittle's crews training for their Tokyo raid at a nearby Eglin auxiliary field early in 1942.

With the new base rapidly nearing completion, Koluder was given a job. "It turned out I was the only man in our group halfway familiar with the manual of arms," he claims, "and so I was directed to train the rest with the old Springfield rifles they issued to us. We had the rifles but there wasn't a round of ammunition to be found. Anyway, we had a ball doing the manual of arms while the construction workers busted their butts to make the base livable enough for us to move in.

"At last a detail was formed to put cots and mattresses in the Tyndall barracks. I was in charge. As we set up cots, the painters were finishing their jobs and, in a couple of days, we broke camp and moved on base. While we were settling in, the contractors were screening porches, turning the water on, etc. It took a week for water to get hot."

Despite the hectic times and the multitude of early problems, a semblance of order soon became apparent and the gunnery schools all began turning out students in a remarkably short time. As we have seen, the modest goals of 1941 soon became outdated. Some two years after personnel began arriving at the first training bases, plans formulated by Headquarters AAF in July of 1943 called for an annual production rate of 180,000 gunners to be achieved by March of 1944. Six months later, a total of 214,826 students had graduated. By this time, all seven schools attained a weekly flow of 3,500, equating to an annual production rate of 182,000. Numbers alone, however, do not automatically spell success, and many training deficiencies became apparent as new gunners entered combat units. As a result, training curricula and student criteria came under close scrutiny, with many changes implemented as combat experience dictated. Some of the results were to prove startling.

Before the pinball

4

Securing students for the flexible gunnery training schools created some problems, primarily because mental, physical and technical qualifications were involved. These criteria, stringent in the beginning, had to be modified considerably before the end of World War II. Original planning called for an all-volunteer, elite group, well taught and properly motivated, which would man the multitude of aerial weapons that ensured the safety of American combat bombers against enemy aerial attack.

Combat personnel replacement requirements, characterized by a voracious appetite for more and more trained gunners, required continuous increases in school quotas. Modest in the beginning, these quotas burgeoned as the war continued, and schools found that aerial warfare, especially in the European Theater, was consuming qualified gunners at a rate no one had ever thought possible in the early stages.

It didn't take long for the planners to scrap the volunteer system, and an arbitrary selection program was imposed. It was also found that early physical and mental standards had to be lowered in order to keep up with combat needs, and this, in turn, resulted in graduating personnel of lower all around quality. All the obstructions bedeviling gunnery training did little to improve what was fast becoming unsatisfactory performance by gunners in combat.

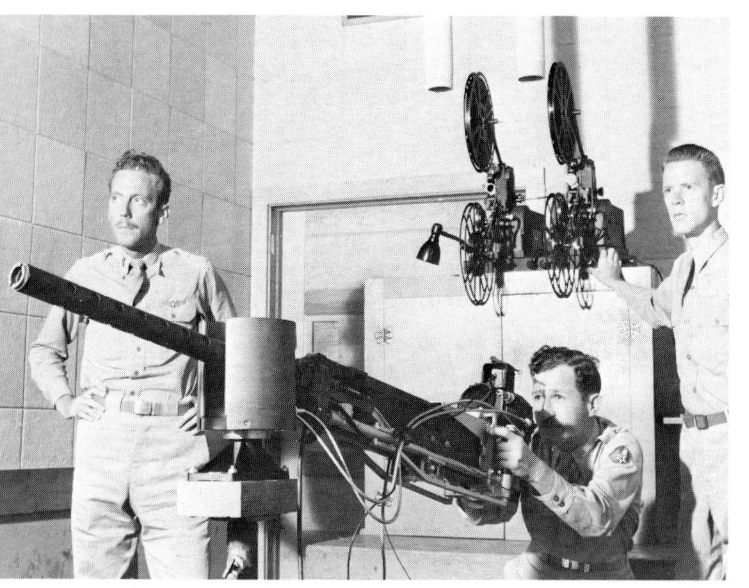

The Jam Handy was the first truly successful synthetic flexible gunnery trainer. Here student aims .50 caliber Browning at aircraft images projected on screen. Note optical sight on machine gun and projectors in rear. Gun was so synchronized that aiming errors were readily noted and scores could be tallied. US Air Force

Another factor affected morale and training efficiency of flexible gunnery school instructors. This was induced by an early program that provided promotions to graduating student gunners. Comparative rank between instructors and students resulted in an intolerable situation that had to be addressed. Instructors, wearing corporal chevrons, were finding themselves outranked by students who, by virtue of early regulations, were promoted to sergeant before shipping off to combat. The situation was exacerbated by the appearance in class of staff and technical sergeants drawn from the ranks of specialists going through training.

As the demand for gunners increased, it became apparent that well-trained instructors, competent officer personnel and proper training equipment were indispensable elements of a successful gunnery training program. The reality was, however, that the instructors were not well-trained. Some were plucked from technical schools and others from the enlisted ranks of flexible gunnery schools. This was obviously an unsatisfactory method.

The original instructors' school was established at Buckingham. Later, a gunnery officers' school was located at the same Florida base but was moved to Laredo due to complaints that Buckingham facilities were inadequate. It is indeed ironic that both schools wound up at this south Texas location.

At any rate, in August of 1942, Headquarters, AAF, directed that enlisted instructors be provided the same promotional opportunities gunnery students enjoyed, and instructor morale improved significantly.

During this comparatively early period, headquarters initiated a system for each instructor to carry a class of students through all phases and subjects of the course. Some liked it, some didn't. Joseph Koluder was among those who did. "Five of us 'brainier' types got together," he recalls, "and set up what was then called the 'flight system' of instruction. It all boiled down to one instructor taking a class, or platoon, of men through the entire course, thus eliminating the wasted time of marching from classroom to classroom and exchanging instructors so many times a day. We were certain the system of giving one man control of the entire group would enable the instructor to help the slow learners and increase the volume of knowledge to graduates.

"Armed with our plan," Koluder says, "we went to the chief honcho, a lieutenant colonel. He loved the idea. He told us that another gunnery school, soon to open at Ft. Myers, Florida (Buckingham Army Air Field), was going to take our idea and see how it worked out. Anyway, the 'flight system' turned out to be a smash hit. The men knew what it was all about when they finished and the competition between individual instructors to bring in the top class added to the value of the instruction."

In the end, the 'flight system' was abandoned. It had both advantages and disadvantages but it soon became clear that it was nearly impossible for each instructor to properly prepare himself in all the diverse phases of flexible gunnery training.

Gunnery experts considered synthetic trainers a valuable aid to the flexible gunnery program from the very beginning. As early as the fall of 1941, the investigating team in England reported on some thirteen synthetic devices used by the Royal Air Force. The British program included a combination of panoramic trainers, spotlight trainers and platform trainers, in addition to the familiar aerial gunnery missions where students fired at towed targets. The team concluded that some trainers had merit and others did not, and it recommended that a board of officers be established to study and evaluate all trainers then in existence.

Two trainers were accepted for use in the gunnery courses, the Jam Handy, a stand-by in the Air Force gunnery program throughout the war, and a later modification, the Waller.

The Jam Handy employed a gun camera, the same type used in aerial missions to simulate combat firing, mounted on a machine gun the student aimed and "fired" at moving aircraft images on a movie screen. It

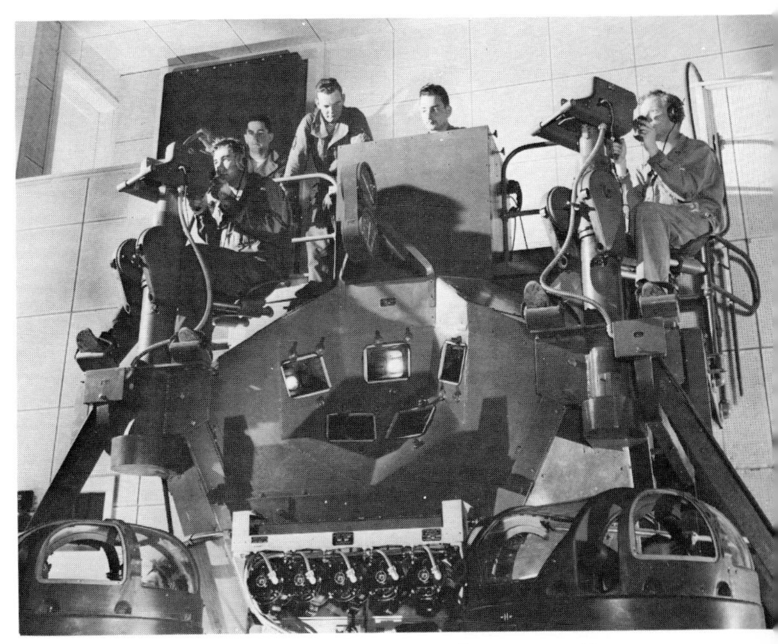

Paraphernalia of the Waller trainer. Note that four students are currently training, two in turrets and two at units similar to remote aiming devices carried by the B-29. Although student was seated, these positions were also used to train gunners for the waist gun positions. Instructors on dais monitor students' performance. Smithsonian Institution

Another version of the Jam Handy trainer. Here two sighting stations are segregated in special enclosures with projectors above. Many different models were used, all seeking the elusive object of providing realism for the embryo gunner.

Simple but effective, the Jam Handy was used by flexible gunnery schools throughout World War II. Smithsonian Institution

View of the panoramic Waller screen on which realistic aerial battle scenes were projected. Heads of two students can be seen operating remote aiming devices. US Air Force

incorporated a built-in means of accurately indicating the student's point of aim and where it should have been.

The Jam Handy was the progenitor of the Waller trainers. Waller Trainer locations were easily identified by the odd-shaped buildings designed around the large screens which, like the Jam Handy, were used to project moving images of aircraft. The Waller was much more sophisticated and realistic than the Jam Handy. The Jam Handy, however, was portable and could be moved at will as the occasion demanded. Many of the Waller buildings may still be seen at defunct flexible gunnery training bases around the country.

A shortage of gunnery-training aircraft lasted well into 1944 and prompted a recommendation by a training conference at Fort Worth that fighter airplanes be earmarked for flexible gunnery training on a high priority basis. The assistant secretary of war for air responded with a criticism of the flexible gunnery program, and this prompted some acidulous exchanges. Flying Training Command, assuming the foremost role in the continuing dichotomy, pointed out that the main problem involving the lack of airplanes lay in the War Department's insistence on assigning increasing numbers of bombers and fighters to combat areas, thus relegating the training mission to a strictly secondary role.

In the end, the War Department relented and assigned more fighters for training. During the latter half of 1944, the situation at all flexible gunnery training bases improved dramatically. The powers that be finally recognized the obvious: People had to be trained in order to fulfill a combat mission.

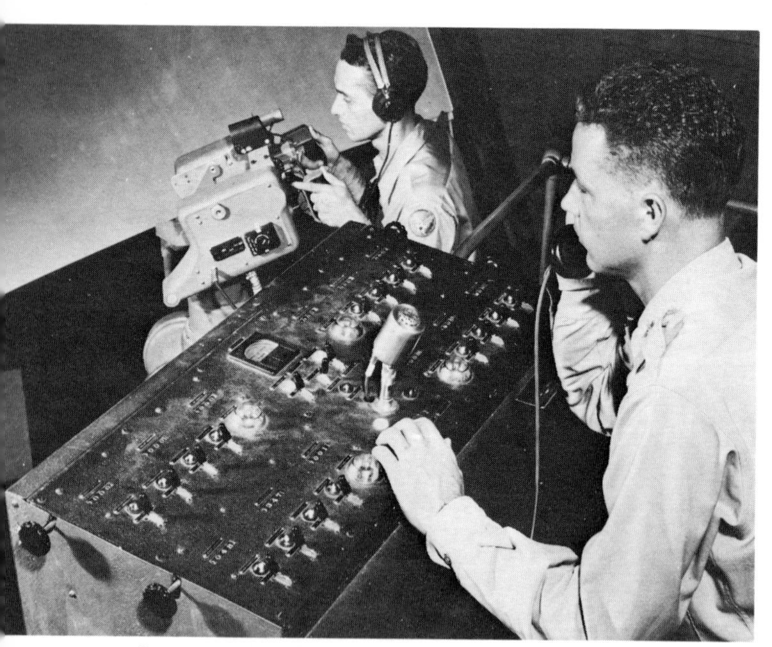

Instructor at control panel of Waller trainer. Student in background is operating remote aiming device. Smithsonian Institution

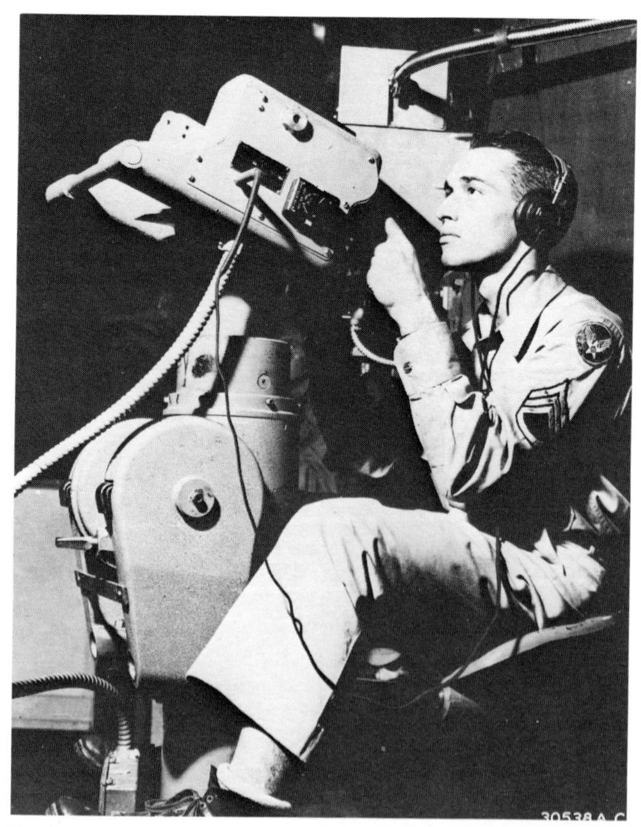

Student manning remote aiming device of Waller trainer. Student is a staff sergeant, obviously a specialist undergoing training in grade. Smithsonian Institution

Doing time in the Texan

During the first year of the two I spent at Kingman Army Air Field, I flew the AT-6, a 550 hp single-engined trainer designed and built by North American Aviation. Now this was a nice airplane, easy to fly (albeit a holy terror on landings, short coupled and with narrow gear). However, as a newly commissioned pilot with visions of high-performance fighters dancing in my head, I was more than a little disappointed to find myself ensconced, once again, in the same, tame little aircraft I had reason to believe I had shed when I finished my abbreviated tour of instructing.

I retain vivid memories of the AT-6 gunnery missions at this desert outpost. Up at 5 a.m., a seven-mile drive from the city of Kingman to the field, a perfunctory briefing by the squadron operations officer, a change to flying togs, meet a student at an assigned aircraft, brief the student, then off into the wild blue in trail formation with five other airplanes. This was the routine six days a week (we did have Sunday off, unless a special mission was called). We flew four missions a day on the firing ranges located south of Yucca, a sub-base some 30 miles southwest of Kingman. And they were full days, *believe me!* Many times in the winter it was dark before I arrived back home at the end of the day. It wasn't all peaches and cream, although I found myself imagining that there must have been a lot of combat pilots who would have gladly changed places with those of us living the life of Riley here stateside.

At first the duty wasn't all that bad. Here we flew from the front cockpit and we all managed to sharpen our flying skills to a great extent. It was all so new: a yammering machine gun in the rear cockpit was something we hadn't encountered before, and then there were the Hualpai Mountains to play around in on our way back from Yucca. Flying down canyons, zooming up over the rims of sheer walls was exhilarating to say the least, however illegal and dangerous it might have been.

The awful boredom eventually set in, and it became a painful chore just to report for duty. And then there was the abominable heat! Anyone who has ever spent a summer in the desert can understand that operating an airplane in that climate could become downright uncomfortable. There was a tendency to don shorts during daytime activities (dress regulations out there were very informal and it was not uncommon to view pilots in various stages of dishabille), but one touch of bare flesh to an overheated aluminum surface could change one's mind in a hurry. We always climbed to maximum altitude after takeoff, just to cool off a trifle. The field elevation was slightly over 3,000 feet and we usually tried for 10,000 on our way to and from Yucca. That altitude produced some relief.

There were some interesting interludes, not all of them pleasant. There was the time they put some of us in B-17s as co-pilots, an unpleasant fate for a confirmed single-fan throttle jockey. And then they shanghaied some more of us for similar duty in the AT-23s. Now, that wasn't so bad. The '23 was a mighty fine airplane with superior performance. There were occasional instrument training sessions and check rides in various types of aircraft, such as the twin-engined AT-11 and the Lockheed AT-18.

But it was the AT-6 to which we were wedded for one long year, and it didn't improve our dispositions or morale one bit to see those female pilots, the storied WASPS (Women Airforce Service Pilots) who flew for the Ferry Command, come wheeling into Kingman in hot fighters like the P-38 or the P-51. I remember this one gal who was ferrying a B-17. She had a captain for co-pilot! We saw a lot of these WASPS because Kingman was a handy refueling point on their frequent trips east from the west coast factories. We always felt they were actually snickering at all of us poor lieutenants stuck with the ludicrous role of hauling student gunners around in something as archaic as an AT-6. In that day the word "chauvinism" was practically unknown and you can bet most of us let the girls know just how we felt about this obscene injustice.

Of course, aircraft were only a part of flexible gunnery training facilities. Classrooms played a significant role in the program, and here, too, differences of opinion existed.

The initial curricula planning for the flexible gunnery training program was the handiwork of Major W. L. Kennedy, of the original RAF study team, and Colonel Delman T. Spivey. They were responsible, more than any others, for getting ground training off on the right foot, and they continued to contribute, mostly in advisory roles, as the program matured.

Kennedy devised the first four-week course at Harlingen and helped prepare the textbooks originally used at that base. Spivey, project officer at Buckingham, did essentially the same thing for that station. Other schools already in operation and those in the process of being established drew heavily on the initial work of these two individuals and, after a time, curricula and texts became standardized at all locations.

Joseph Koluder instructed in the first training exercises at Tyndall. He remembers them well: "We got our assignments in a pretty informal manner. One man would teach aerial tracking, another the .30 caliber machine gun, with various other items assigned somewhat haphazardly. When we started classes, people were marching from class to class the whole damned day. We were teaching ranks and grades from colonel to private, and nationalities as diverse as Poles and Argentineans. I was given the task of teaching 'yaw,' the deviation of leading and trailing edges of a projectile along its arc of trajectory toward a target. I used to chuckle when I said 'yaw' and watch jaws drop to chests. I never could figure out why they had that in the course.

"My other job," Koluder recalls, "was dropping targets for those sent up for air-to-air firing. Our pilots were flying sergeants in the early days of the war, and I think they only came out to fly to sober up. Anyway, I

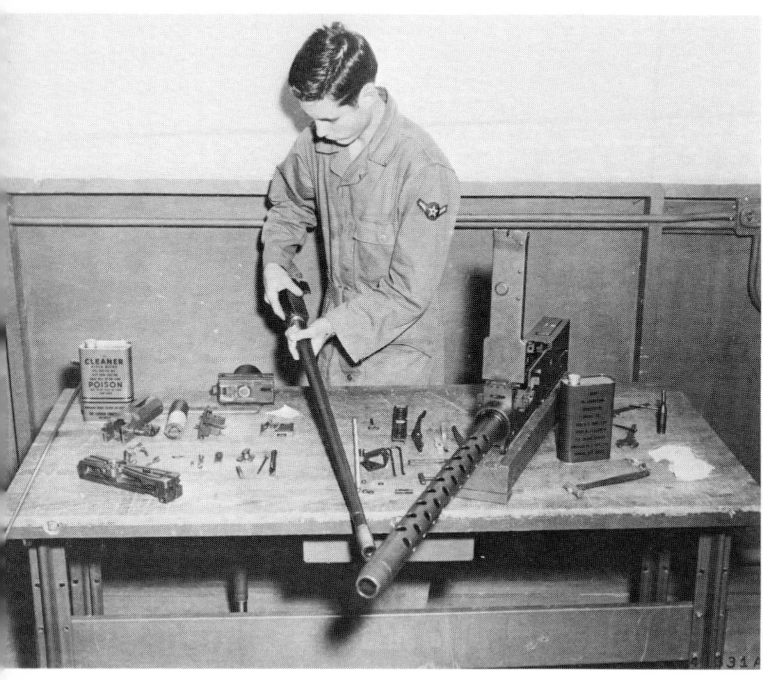

Disassembling the .50 caliber Browning in the classroom. Student gunners spent many hours in this vital training, designed to impart knowledge and skills that came in handy many times in crucial combat situations. Smithsonian Institution

got a lot of stick time. I believe the airplanes were B-34s. [They were.] I would kick out a target and if it stayed on the cable, let the gunners fire away. After one group finished we would fly back over the base and drop one target, using a new target to release the shot up (sometimes) sleeve." (The Army discontinued using enlisted pilots relatively early in World War II. Sergeant pilots were all eventually commissioned, usually as

A class in .50 caliber machine gun nomenclature at Laredo AAF. This segment of ground training occupied a substantial part of the gunnery students' curriculum. Smithsonian Institution

flight officers. This was a wartime rank comparable to warrant officer. Promotion from flight officer was to second lieutenant.)

Among the many changes that were to occur in flexible gunnery training was increased emphasis on range exercises and firing. The course length was eventually increased from four to six weeks with an attendant increase in hours of instruction. One of the imperatives brought to light by combat experience was the incorporation of oxygen management training at high altitude.

Of course, guns occupied a large part of ground school training. Contrary to popular belief, a great many students demonstrated only a rudimentary knowledge of guns, even shotguns or the more commonplace .22 caliber rifle. It became necessary to institute a familiarization course in basic weapons before progressing to the more complicated machine gun. Training bases were short-changed early on in the allocation of these weapons, both .30 caliber and the newer .50 caliber. Ammunition, especially the .50 caliber, was in short supply and for a time, all firing exercises—both ground and aerial—were accomplished with the smaller .30 caliber. Of course, in the early days all air-to-air firing was from AT-6s, and this small trainer was not stressed for the heavier weapon. Later, in 1943, Training Command was able to incorporate .50 caliber aerial firing using bombers as gun platforms and AT-23s for towing targets.

The AT-23, a training version of the Martin B-26, was used extensively at all of the flexible gunnery bases. Some were confiscated by base commanders and used for "official" transportation, although such shenanigans weren't widely advertised. The AT-23 was a very fast airplane, which probably accounts for its popularity with the brass. Pilots who flew the plane became very unhappy when assigned to any other type.

Aircraft identification became especially important to gunners. Great emphasis was placed on this phase during training. An early system assumed the acronym WEFT, which stood for Wings, Engines, Fuselage and Tail, all separate entities to harassed crew members trying to identify an approaching aircraft as either hostile or friendly. Each student was expected to become familiar with German, Japanese, Italian, Russian, English and American aircraft, based on WEFT parameters, and commit to memory shapes, numbers and sizes of various airplane components. WEFT proved unsatisfactory for obvious reasons—mainly because it required the gunner to concentrate on too many things during the extremely short time he had to identify an aircraft and, if necessary, take steps to shoot down the attacker.

It stood to reason that sooner or later an easier system had to come. Samuel Renshaw of the Department of Experimental Psychology at Ohio State University came up with a method that filled the bill nicely. Called the Renshaw system after the originator, it soon became referred to as the "flash" method and it became standard for both branches of the service. The US

Skeet shooting from mounted 12-gauge shotguns. Note machine gun-type handles and remote triggers. Officers and airmen, as shown here, were intermingled and trained together. This type gunnery training was, at best, of dubious value. US Air Force

Naval Training School in Aircraft Recognition was established at Ohio State in 1942 using the Renshaw system. Many Air Force officers, mostly from the Flying Training Command, entered the school later in the year; their enthusiasm was largely responsible for incorporating "flash" into the flexible gunnery training curriculum.

The "flash" method recognized the fallacy of trying to identify aircraft merely by nationality. (Witness the many instances of enemy crews operating captured Allied aircraft.) It stressed aircraft tactics and probable intent in preference to visual acuity. The Air Force officially adopted the Renshaw system in 1943. The new system resulted in reducing aircraft recognition training hours from an exorbitant twenty to a modest ten in 1944.

Throughout World War II the Air Force devoted much thought and experimentation to the elusive prob-

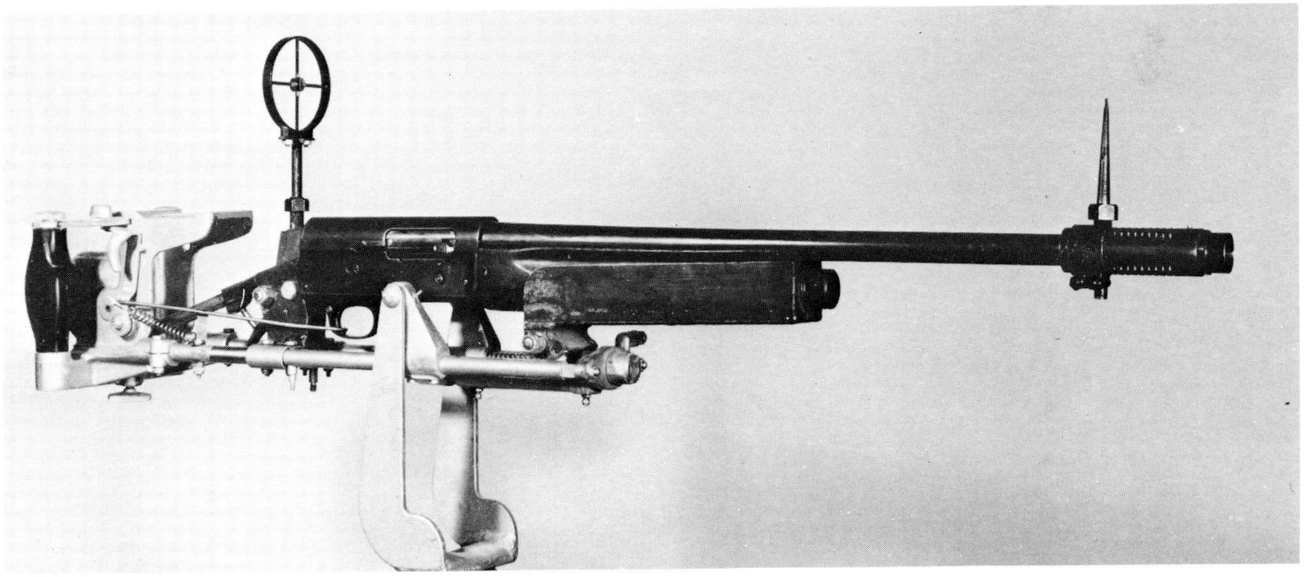

The Browning 12-gauge automatic shotgun as it was adapted for skeet shooting from a pedestal. With this adaptation, stock has been replaced with machine gun-type handles. Note crude remote trigger. This gun was used at Las Vegas AAF. Smithsonian Institution

lem of downing attacking aircraft. Many training methods were employed, some as bizarre as using shotguns against clay pigeons, with the assumption that if a gunner could bring down a clay target with a handheld weapon on the ground, that gunner could do the same with a machine gun against a swiftly moving aircraft in the air.

There were the synthetic trainers, of course, and in an effort to approximate the equipment carried aloft by our bombers, guns and turrets were mounted on trucks and towers from which students "fired" cameras at aircraft making simulated, low-level passes. The target airplanes, mostly Stearman PT-13s and Vultee BT-13s and -15s, were slow, two-seat trainers used at that time for primary and basic flying training.

These aircraft entered the program at a relatively late date and each training base had to use assigned pilots to ferry them in. Some interesting experiences resulted, like the one related by Barrie Davis who was then stationed at Las Vegas. "In March of 1945," he recalls, "several of us went to a primary flying school (Ontario, California, I think) and picked up some PT-13s. We hadn't flown Stearmans since flying school but the civilian instructors got us current with one circuit of the traffic pattern. The flying cadets watched in awe as we bounced and bounded all over the runway. The sight should have given them supreme confidence in the rugged strength of the Stearman.

"We nearly froze crossing the hills on our return to Vegas. Without radios, we decided to fly formation down the runway to announce our arrival. We bounced and tossed against a pretty fair headwind for what seemed like an eternity before we crossed the far boundary of the field. I remember making three more flights in the PT-13 before moving north to Indian Springs. [Fighter Operations moved to that sub-base just prior to starting the pinball missions in April.] I never knew why those PT-13s were brought to Las Vegas."

One phase of training involved shotguns mounted in turrets from which students fired at clay pigeons on the ground range. Mounted on trucks, the turrets were designed to give the embryo gunner a feel for hydraulically moving his weapon and, at the same time, provide practice in estimating lead of a target.

Another interesting experiment was moving base trapshooting. Here students rode in the beds of pickup trucks, firing at clay pigeons thrown at different angles from various locations around a racetrack circuit. The

Various small aircraft were used for gunnery training. Here a Stearman PT-17 makes a simulated attack against students "firing" cameras from a tower at Buckingham Army Air Field. Student gunners also used turrets to track these "attacking" aircraft. US Air Force

vehicles usually moved at a steady twenty mph and gave the student practice in determining lead from a moving station to a moving target. This type of trapshooting declined later with the introduction of skeet ranges, but great differences of opinion remained regarding the value of shotguns in teaching a student how to track and fire a machine gun. One thing is sure: the moving base provided hours of entertainment for those saddled with the otherwise boring duty of ground range officer. The facility was available when no students were scheduled, and many pilots became quite adept at this form of trapshooting.

Harold Ericsson recalls the moving base training at Las Vegas with some nostalgia. "I remember this round (sic) track," he says, "and as we drove around it in the back of a pickup, they'd throw clay pigeons at us from towers at ground level and at various angles. We'd shoot at these clay pigeons with shotguns. Another thing we did was shoot at ground targets from what I believe were B-29 top turrets. I believe they had four guns in them—at least I remember they put out an awful lot of lead." [Top turrets carried two .50 caliber machine guns.]

Ernest (Ernie) R. McDowell went through gunnery school as a bombardier cadet and, in later years, authored a number of fine military aviation books. He provides some fascinating details of early flexible gunnery training efforts, most from his own extensive experience, the rest from friends and acquaintances. His recollection of ground firing at Laredo is especially interesting. An excerpt from his letter follows:

"As I recall, we had the Sperry ball, Martin and Sperry uppers, Consolidated tail and Emerson nose turrets in which we had to take turns sitting in on the ground to get the feel . . . learn where the operating controls were located, what sights they had and how to use them. They had some mounted on platforms in front of a hemisphere screen and we were supposed to track moving silhouettes of aircraft projected on the screens. These things seem to have been the inspiration for the Waller trainer that came along later and, after the war, for Cinerama. The final result of this type simulator was a close approximation to actual combat with movies of real aircraft coming at you from various angles of attack and you naturally were to track and 'shoot' the enemy aircraft down. If you fired when out of range, a bell rang; if in range the ring sight was superimposed on the screen over the one in the movie if you were leading correctly. Conversely, it would be way the hell off it if your lead were incorrect. [This was

Turret training encompassed a variety of modes and methods. Here a gunnery student is engaged in a form of automated skeet using a shotgun to fire at clay targets. The effectiveness of this program was hotly debated throughout World War II. Smithsonian Institution

Students learned to use the .50 caliber machine gun in turrets, firing at both stationary and moving targets. Turrets were complex pieces of equipment and students had difficulty learning to operate them. Note the ever-present instructors who observed actual firing closely. US Air Force

an update of the Jam Handy trainer and a precursor of the sophisticated Waller. Many modifications of synthetic trainers were made. Some were good, some were not.]

"Then there were the turrets mounted on GI trucks. At first they had a shotgun mounted in lieu of the machine gun and one student gunner would man the turret, track the clay pigeon and fire while another student sat on top of the truck cab to load the shotgun after each firing. Apparently the way the shotguns were mounted prevented loading the pump guns in any other manner. It was just about impossible to miss using the sight and the turret.

"Next came real .50 caliber guns and ammo. We fired at a canvas target mounted on a jeep running in a large circular track shielded by high walls of sand. The target, however, was above the sand walls and in plain sight. Again, this was so easy most of us used to try to shoot out one of the four-by-fours holding the target. A good hit used to splinter these thick lumber uprights. The .50 was a very lethal weapon."

Gunsights received a commensurate share of attention and gunnery students were given training on all types then in combat use. In early 1942, students devoted twenty of the total 150 ground training hours to the study of the ring and bead, reflector, compensating and telescopic sights, together with associated factors affecting sighting. These included bullet deflection, relative speeds of opposing aircraft and tracer firing. Of the 288 hours given at that time to the entire gunnery program, forty-four were allotted to sighting, with another eight to range estimation, twelve to the Jam Handy and six to the Waller trainer.

Computing lead proved especially troublesome in classroom situations. During 1942 students were given training on six different types of ring and bead and four types of optical sights. Many methods, using all of the sights, were tried. The Relative Speed System was the first. This involved teaching a cumbersome sequence of sighting actions. The student was expected first to recognize the approaching airplane as friend or foe, then to estimate the range (600 yards being the critical distance from which to open fire), estimate the difference in speed between his ship and the target by holding the sight stationary for one second (are you following all of this?), compute lead according to a definite table to be memorized, and finally to open fire.

The Relative Speed System required a student to apply a scientific method of problem solving. Undoubtedly, it was the brainchild of some over-educated egghead who had never seen a machine gun, much less fired one. The wonder is that our high-level brass would even consider such a preposterous system. We had some clear-thinking generals in the Air Force at that time (General George Kenney comes immediately to mind) who would have made short shrift of such non-

Turret training included night firing on ground-to-ground ranges. Here student's twin .50s provide spectacular show at Las Vegas AAF. Turret appears to be modification of the Martin upper (minus plexiglass cover) used on the B-17. Smithsonian Institution

sense, but unfortunately General Kenney was not then in a policy-making position. To the knowledgeable, using the scientific approach, no target could possibly be in sight by the time a gunner had gone through such an involved process.

Aerial gunnery training proved less than effective in the overall scheme. Carrying a student armed with a single .30 caliber machine gun aloft in the rear seat of an AT-6 trainer was the archaic method originally employed; it remained the primary aerial gunnery training tool well into 1944. In retrospect, this was practically worthless as a training device. Well aware of the system's deficiencies, top-level planners retained it for the dubious benefit the student might obtain in the form of air experience. They exhibited little concern over whether or not the student might incur anything to stand him in good stead when the chips were down.

To some young men exposed to flight for the first time in their lives, the experience of firing a machine gun from a precarious perch in a bouncing little airplane could be quite unsettling. Some macho types, of course, became barracks heroes by recounting their derring-do exploits in the air, and some (though not many) displayed extraordinary skill in hitting an airborne target.

Students were supposed to be briefed on emergencies and intercom procedures by the pilot prior to each airborne mission. This briefing by some young, bored throttle jockey (and there were no standardized procedures at the time) was usually cursory in nature. Psychological factors, likely to adversely affect the embryo gunner, were seldom considered, and pilots generally had little patience with a frightened youngster cringing in the rear cockpit.

These aerial gunnery missions were usually conducted by formations of five or six AT-6s, each carrying one student. The gunners fired at a cloth sleeve or banner target towed behind a bomber, usually a B-17 or a B-34. Stepped up in echelon opposite the target, the trainers would assume a parallel position with the towing aircraft and each in turn would move into firing position opposite to and in range of the sleeve or banner. At this time, the gunner was required to rise from a seated position (many times only after urgent persuasion by the pilot), aim his weapon and fire at the target until he expended his 100 rounds of ammunition. The firing aircraft would then peel off and fall in at the rear of his formation.

Ernie McDowell had his share of aerial gunnery. "The next step after ground gunnery was firing at a sleeve from a real turret," he writes. "I only fired from Martin and Sperry uppers during the course, although my first aerial gunnery firing was actually a few missions in the rear seat of an AT-6 with a .30 caliber gun, facing backwards (during the trip to and from the range) and firing when my turn came at a towed sleeve that looked like a cigarette in the distance . . . and not even king size! [Firing from bombers at targets towed by AT-23s and B-34s was a later development in aerial gunnery training.] My class was the first to go through

The Spotlight was a modification of the Jam Handy in which students tracked visual images on a large screen with a turret. Turrets in training were nearly identical to those used in combat, except that plexiglass covers were normally removed for the comfort of the gunner. The Spotlight, using electronic means to monitor students' tracking ability, was an effective trainer. Smithsonian Institution

The moving target vehicle. Students fired at cloth target with .50 caliber machine guns. The lethal .50 caliber many times completely destroyed the 4x4 posts holding the target aloft. Bullet hole colors identified individual gunners. Smithsonian Institution

Students first fire live ammunition from fixed machine guns, beginning with .30 caliber Brownings (four on far left), progressing to the larger .50 calibers. Note the sandbags used to hold platforms steady. The recoil of a .50 caliber was not insignificant. Ever-present instructors keep watchful eyes on live firing. US Air Force

The burst control range in action. Here students were taught judicious fire control. Many veterans described the tendency to "freeze" on the gun trigger, wasting ammunition and disrupting aim. Smithsonian Institution

gunnery without using tracer bullets. We did get to fire some tracers on the range at night—just once. The theory was that with tracers gunners tended to 'hose' the target rather than aim and lead properly, and would thus fire much longer bursts than desired. Also, by missing the first shots, they would alert the enemy to the fact he was being fired on. I imagine a hell of a lot of gunners, in the heat of combat, would forget everything and hose away until they ran out of ammo."

During World War II, brass was considered a critical metal and the US government was continually

Student gunners firing .30 caliber machine guns at night make a spectacular display at Harlingen Army Air Field. Much experimentation with tracer took place during World War II. At the time of this photo (1944), one of five rounds was tracer. US Air Force

Students received thorough instruction on various types of compensating sights. Here instructor explains the workings of the K-11. Note that instructor wears gunner's wings and is only a private first class. Inequities in rank caused much dissatisfaction among instructors until these important individuals were properly recognized. Smithsonian Institution

Student gunner behind a .30 caliber machine gun in the rear seat of an AT-6. Ammunition fed from metal container on left side with another on the opposite side to catch the links. Note the canvas bag on bottom designed to pick up spent cartridge casings. US Air Force

Three AT-6s carrying students on a training mission at Laredo Army Air Field. Sleeve targets (banners were also used) were towed by a variety of aircraft, usually B-17s or B-34s. US Air Force

reminding everyone to conserve this precious commodity. The machine guns carried by the AT-6s had a canvas chute attached to catch and save expended shell casings for reprocessing. This brings to mind a humorous incident that's supposed to have occurred at Buckingham early in the gunnery training program.

Charles Pierce was commander of a training squadron there from the spring of 1943 to the summer of 1945. One of his AT-6 pilots, flying a gunnery mission one day, noticed that his gunner was losing a lot of shell casings. He called his student on interphone and told him to save his brass. Evidently the student thought the pilot said "Save your ass" and promptly bailed out. The story is sworn to be true (no proof) and if so, it proves that at least a part of the preflight briefing (that is, use of the parachute in an emergency) was effective.

The subject of tracer has always been controversial; there are as many opponents as proponents of the concept which began in World War I. Tracers were pretty well eliminated toward the end of the first great conflict because most felt they gave a distorted impression of just where the bullets were going. However, because of much higher flight speeds during World War II, many believed that tracer sighting discrepancies could be greatly reduced if tracers were used in conjunction with other modes. Tests were run in many configurations, but the arguments over the viability of tracer firing continued without a consensus.

After students had received instruction in ground gunnery firing, the perplexing aerial phase soon demonstrated that firing at objects on the ground proved considerably different from shooting at targets from a moving aircraft or tracking an "attacking" fighter with camera guns. Completely different sets of values applied, and although moving base ranges did much to adapt gunners to dissimilar types of firing, only the aerial phase provided the environment to give the student the experience needed when subjected to actual combat.

Computing sights, crude by modern standards, were in use on B-17s and B-24s, as well as the more advanced B-29s, throughout the war. The early ones

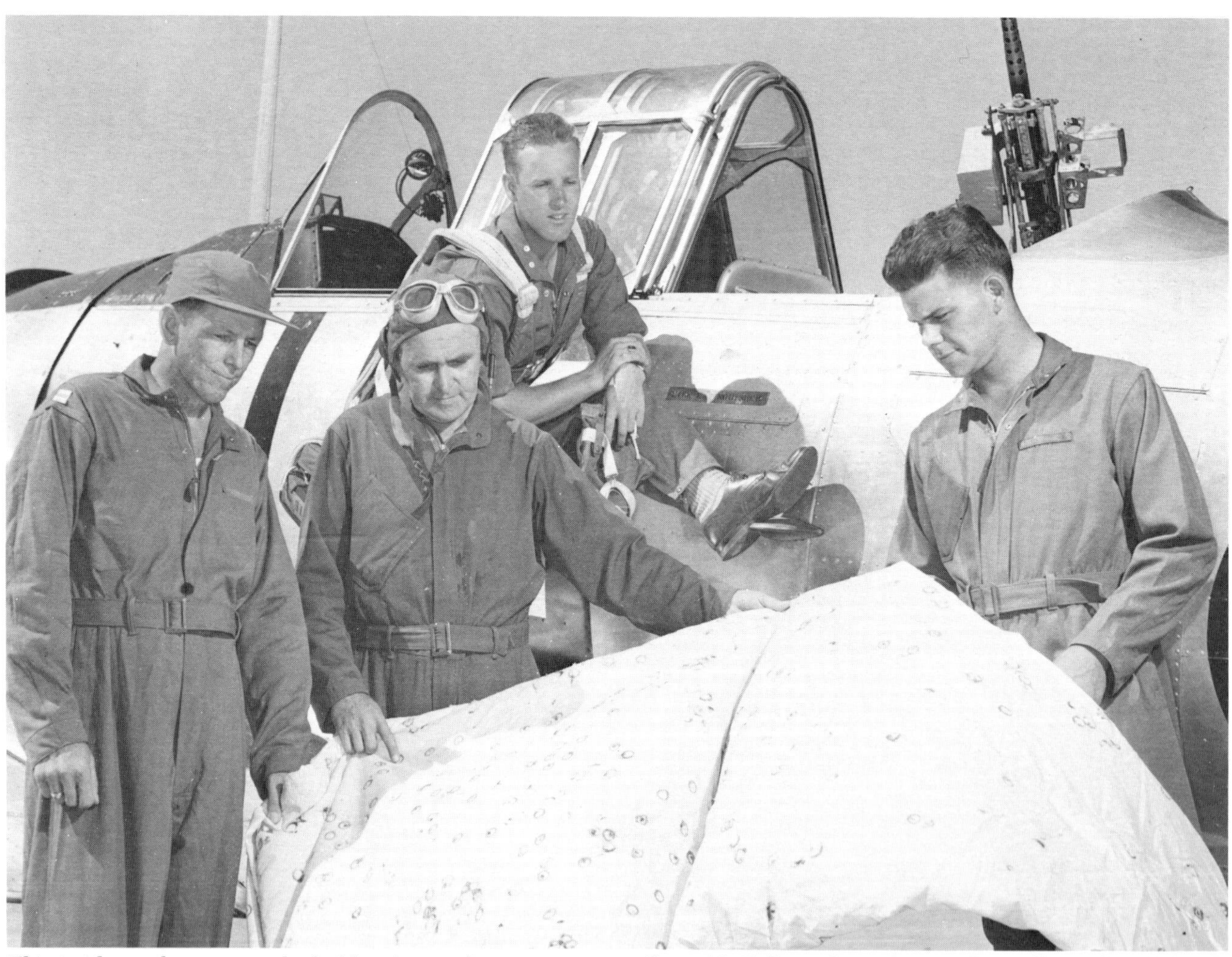

This is what a sleeve target looks like after student gunners complete a firing mission. This one has been well "clobbered." Interested Laredo AAF pilots shown here are (L to R) Capt. McCullum, Capt. Presser, Lt. Friller and Lt. Schwab. US Air Force

The gunsight computer used in the B-29. This is just a fraction of the total equipment needed to control the automatic gun tracking system of this preeminent World War II bomber. Archaic by today's standards (the transistor and chip had not yet been developed, of course), this electronic marvel made the B-29 a superior aircraft for its time but was bulky, heavy and awkward to handle. General Curtis LeMay, commander of the Ninth Air Force, removed the equipment and most of the B-29's defensive armament in order to carry larger bomb loads on night missions against Japan. The B-29s retained only their tail guns and losses due to enemy fighters were minimal. Smithsonian Institution

left much to be desired. Initial development resulted in the Sperry K-13 which was expedited for use in the flexible gunnery schools. A follow-up, the K-15, was used by the navy for training purposes beginning in August of 1944. In November the sight was installed in the Martin turrets of B-24s and finally, in February of 1945, in the Sperry turrets of B-17s and in the Sperry ball turrets of B-24s.

The General Electric computing sight, developed later and used on B-29s, was much better but it too had its flaws. It was the remote turret aiming device on the Superfortress. However, these engineering marvels, sophisticated as they were in their day and advertised as the ultimate defensive devices of aerial warfare, proved woefully inadequate against Japanese fighters managing to reach the altitudes at which the B-29s first operated. When LeMay opted for low-level incendiary missions over Japan, he eliminated the remote system and the associated heavy, cumbersome electronic equipment, leaving only tail guns for protection. It remained for modern-day airborne radar to provide effective defensive firepower for larger aircraft.

The most significant development in gunnery training prior to the latter stages of the war was gun camera missions, beginning in the summer of 1944. Regarded as the system most nearly approximating combat conditions, it quickly gained favor as the ultimate in gunnery training, despite widespread dissemination of news about a new, more realistic program being developed at Duke University. To conduct the gun camera missions, AN (Army-Navy) gun cameras were installed on machine guns at various locations on

This photo shows officers assessing camera film. Instruments were used to determine whether student's aim was proper. Here two instructors are obviously viewing some shots without benefit of assessment equipment. This is not a fighter "attacking" in a curve of pursuit. It could very well be film taken by a fighter pilot engaged in some extracurricular dogfighting. Smithsonian Institution

bomber aircraft. With these cameras students tracked and photographed fighters making curves of pursuit passes against them. Film exposed during the missions would then be developed and run through an assessing device which theoretically would indicate whether hits were being made, and thus evaluate a student's performance.

(To understand the mechanics of a curve of pursuit, visualize a fighter aircraft and its target, usually a bomber in formation, flying parallel to each other and with the fighter higher and slightly ahead of but out of range of the bomber's defensive armament. To initiate the curve, the fighter starts turning into his target, reversing the direction of turn when he has obtained the proper lead with his sight. He maintains and gradually reduces his lead as his angle of closure decreases and, in combat, starts firing when in proper range. Dropping back behind the bomber at minimum angle-off, he would take evasive action in combat, but in the case of flexible gunnery training, he would continue his turn, distancing himself for another pass.)

At the time gun cameras were introduced, fighter pilots were returning from combat and were being used to impart the product of their experience to the fledgling program. These combat veterans had flown actual missions and they knew the mechanics of attack. They fit right in and helped the younger fighter pilots just out of flying schools adapt to combat tactics—which is what the gun camera missions demanded. Gun cameras doomed the towed targets.

This was not the final answer, of course, and planners were soon aware of some significant drawbacks. There was the problem of scoring techniques, never really standardized throughout Training Command. In addition, introduction of the system necessitated a concurrent and extensive increase in photographic functions, resulting in massive additions of training personnel and equipment. The majority agreed, however, that advantages outweighed disadvantages and gun camera training enjoyed a high level of confidence right up to the end of hostilities.

Gun camera mounted on a .50 caliber machine gun in the waist of a B-17 at Kingman Army Air Field. This combination came into being with the advent of gun camera missions in 1944. Note the crude front bead sight. US Air Force

The problems with turrets 5

Flying at high altitude and beset by enemy aircraft attacking from all quarters, gunners quickly found problems entirely different from those encountered on the ground ranges of training bases. Accuracy up there under abnormal atmospheric conditions suffered, even with hand-held guns. With the complex duties involved in operating a turret, things became even more complicated. Turrets had now become a necessity and many factors had to be considered. Appropriate sights had to be installed, power to operate the turrets had to be provided and the whole delicate mechanism had to be kept in balance.

Gunners remember well the importance of turret operation and maintenance. They can relate in graphic detail those instances where knowledge of turret mechanics figured in their being able to put a malfunctioning apparatus back in operation, many times when the survival of a bomber desperately depended on their skill and ability.

Combat experiences emphasized the importance of this phase of gunnery training, and between 1942 and 1943 the hours allotted to turret maintenance and manipulation were increased from thirty-five to fifty. Included in the maintenance phase was: installation and boresighting of the guns; mounting sights; checking and understanding the operation of fire interrupters; understanding the mechanics of the turret, guns and sights; and the loading of ammunition. In the second phase, students were taught to operate the machinery, including sight adjustment; to properly enter and exit the turret (gunners found this one of the more important lessons); to locate and use all switches, interphone and oxygen connections; and to engage and disengage all clutches. These were, indeed, complicated pieces of machinery. Remote-controlled turrets did not come into use until the B-29 was introduced into combat late in the war.

The year 1942 was considered an experimental period. Efforts to improve turret instruction, in the absence of definitive experience and guidelines, was as groping and tentative as all other phases of gunnery training. A shortage of parts was especially serious. Almost all the problems involved in teaching students how to operate turrets were caused by the priority given to combat operations. Complaints from the war theaters resulted in this kind of false economy. Training Command replied by pointing out that all the equipment in the world would prove useless without trained personnel to operate it.

On June 25, 1942, Major General Barton K. Yount, commanding general of Army Air Forces Training Command, reminded Headquarters AAF that although the anticipated output of trained gunners approximated 2,000 per month, there was not *one* airplane equipped with a turret in any of the gunnery schools. Even after turrets became available, the effect of altitude on turret operation remained serious. This involved malfunctions, multiplied by the extremely cold temperatures high in the earth's atmosphere. This made adjusting guns and gun solenoids and reloading ammunition extremely difficult. During the latter part of 1942, AAF directed Flying Training Command to concentrate on high altitude flying, with primary emphasis on the use and adjustment of oxygen equipment.

In early 1943, six types of turrets became available for gunnery training. They were the Consolidated tail turret, the Sperry upper and lower turrets, the Martin upper turret, and the Bendix upper and lower turrets. Each differed significantly from the others, adding greatly to the problem of turret indoctrination.

This example of nonstandardization led to the specialization principle later in 1943, when specific types of turrets were assigned to different schools. Initially, Laredo and Harlingen used nothing but B-24 bombers and restricted training to only the turrets carried by that

The E-5 trainer consisted of a Consolidated tail turret mounted on a truck. This turret, which did yeoman service defending B-24s, was used extensively in training. Many students reported difficulty entering and exiting the turret. US Air Force

aircraft. Similarly, Las Vegas and Kingman were equipped only with the B-17 while Tyndall employed almost equal numbers of B-26s and B-34s. Buckingham had a ratio of sixty percent B-26s and B-34s, while the remaining forty percent consisted of light and dive bombardment types. (Yuma had not yet converted to gunnery training.) In the beginning, graduates from the first four schools (heavy bombardment) were sent to the Second Air Force with those from Tyndall and Buckingham directed to the Third.

Problems in the specialization program cropped up almost immediately. Gunners trained on one type of turret many times were assigned to units using aircraft with entirely different equipment. This brought about some modifications in 1944, when the Flexible Gunnery Instructors School at Laredo (remember, this school was originally located at Buckingham) began training students in all types of turrets. In February the decision was made to return thirty percent of the instructor graduates to their original stations and the remainder to the air forces. The largest share of those heading for combat units (fifty percent) were allocated to B-24s with forty percent to B-17s, four percent each to B-25s and B-26s and the remaining to miscellaneous aircraft units. B-29 allocations were included in those going to B-17s.

In May of 1944, turret instruction was deleted for radio operator mechanics and the same directive assigned all other gunners to the gun position for which they had been trained. However, specialization was further diluted in a Training Command memorandum of May 31, which directed that all gunners be required to become familiar with all of the gun positions on their particular aircraft.

Ernie McDowell had extensive experience with most of the turrets and he identifies the good and bad points of each. They all had different sights and this led to comparisons by the gunners using them. "The one I liked least was the Sperry ball," McDowell says. "It required you to set the wing span into the sight, as I recall, operating a set of reticles by foot pressure which meant (a), you had to identify the enemy aircraft damned fast; (b) you had to constantly adjust the image reticles as he approached or left; and (c) you had to

A familiar face graces this upper turret trainer. Many people are unaware that Clark Gable, at that time at the very height of his popularity and fame, enlisted in the Army Air Force and became a gunner. Lt. Gable is shown here during training at Tyndall Army Air Field. Gable entered the service as a private, attended Officer Candidate School and was promoted to first lieutenant while at Tyndall. He later served with the Eighth Air Force in England. Many Air Force documentary and training films were made and produced under Gable's supervision. He participated in a number of bombing missions. US Air Force

A gunner looks back

by C. Joseph Warth

I entered the Air Force in September of 1942, initially to be in the Signal Corps. I was sent to Atlantic City, New Jersey, to attend basic training (my quarters were in the Hotel Traymore, a wonderful place for basic training). There I was given a series of Air Force exams and was offered a chance to become a gunner and earn a set of silver wings in just a few weeks' time. This I jumped at without a second thought, so two weeks after joining the Air Force I was off to Fort Myers, Florida. There I joined a group of 300 more recruits and became part of the class of 42-47.

I graduated twelfth in the class on November 22, 1942, a short two months after entering military service. I was promoted to staff sergeant on December 1, 1942—from the grade of private to staff sergeant in a matter of days.

America was starting to recover from a massive depression that had lasted for almost a decade. World War II started, of course, in September of 1939 with the invasion by Germany of Poland. England, France and Russia entered the fray that would last until May of 1945 in Europe. We here in the states, while not involved directly, had seen some of our friends go across the border to Canada and enlist in the Canadian Air Force. Most became pilots, a few navigators or bomb aimers, and a few gunners. Some of the latter would pass on their skills and knowledge later to benefit our training programs.

Some limited gunnery training programs were proposed and some placed into use by our armed services between the summer of 1939 and our entry into the war in December of 1941. This gave impetus to a massive and complicated training program for several million unskilled, untrained and, in a few cases, unmotivated members of what would become in three short years the largest and most effective military machine in history.

Some statistics may be in order. For numbers to be trained (and we're talking Air Force now) let's consider just one type of aircraft, the B-24 Liberator. Over 19,000 of these heavy bombers were built for just one purpose: bombing Germany and Japan. Italy and North Africa didn't really count; they didn't last that long and the Ploesti raids were really against Germany. To fly the 19,000 aircraft, the Air Force would have to train over 50,000 pilots, 60,000 navigators and bombardiers, 30,000 flight engineers and over 100,000 gunners! Most of the latter would be dual-qualified as radio operators or engineers, and we must not forget the six to eight ground crew personnel required to maintain each plane, another 150,000.

And so a total of almost 400,000 men would have to learn skills foreign to them, unrelated to their civilian skills. And most important to remember, the majority to be trained were just out of high school, a few college trained, in an age category ranging from eighteen to the "old guys" of twenty-two or twenty-three.

Multiply the above figures by ten to account for other types of bombers, fighters and support aircraft, add the numbers to be trained for the rest of the Army, the Navy and Marines, plus all the auxiliary and ancillary troops of the military services and support for our allies, and we have a figure that exceeds 5,000,000 people. And the demand was to train and equip them overnight!

We can now sit back and say, "Why didn't they plan ahead? Why didn't they do this or that?" It boils down to one important point: when we entered the war we had a very limited number of combat experienced personnel to form a training cadre for the school systems that would be training millions.

My initial training was a few short weeks in which I learned how to wear a uniform, hold a gun for the first time, learn the basic orders of the military, take a few tests for eyesight, and the ability to understand a few basic skills, then volunteer to be a gunner. The chances of surviving a tour of combat was, in September of 1942, almost nil, or so we were informed by the grapevine. Few crews at that time had come through unscathed and America's military might was just starting to be felt. Most of the youngsters coming into the Air Force then were like me: ready to go into combat as quickly as possible and also to earn a pair of wings. Gunnery school was the fastest way, so here we were, ready, willing and available!

Soon after I volunteered to become an aerial gunner in Atlantic City, I found myself with several hundred others on a train headed for the unknown, a gunnery school somewhere in the South. After several days backtracking on the hidden railways of America, we arrived at a rail siding in a swampy area we were told was in the state of Florida. Fort Myers, to be exact, where barracks and runways had been built, practically overnight. A military command had been established there to train what would eventually become thousands of raw recruits how to fire and maintain a machine gun, .50 caliber, in a moving aircraft under combat conditions.

Our training was to be provided by instructors who had just graduated in the school's first class, or a very few who had been in the infantry earlier and knew which end of a gun was the destructive end. And the training had to be completed in the shortest time possible in order to provide crews for dozens, later hundreds, of aircraft coming off the assembly lines daily, and to compensate for crew losses in training and combat that would eventually exceed 100 percent of planes and personnel.

From the rail siding we were taken by truck to our barracks where we were introduced to military life—double-deck bunks, roll calls and formations, and issuance of gunnery manuals and other supplies such as flying suits, helmets, goggles and other associated paraphernalia.

So our training commenced. As I remember it was a four-week course, consisting of both ground and aerial training. On the ground our courses included:

1. What a machine gun was, how it worked, how to maintain it and how to use it. (Our arms were to be the .50 caliber machine gun, either mounted in a window or hatch of the airplane or dual guns in a turret.)
2. A little on basic aeronautics and Morse code to provide some idea of what flying was and how to communicate.
3. Ground gunnery on the practice ranges shooting at various targets, learning how to use gunsights, burst

control and instruction on the types of ammo we would be using.

After two weeks or so of ground training, we went to the flight line for our first taste of how to shoot a gun from a plane. Our planes were AT-6s and our pilots were mostly staff sergeants. Most were later replaced by commissioned officers.

The AT-6 was a two-seat trainer, pilot in the front and student gunner in the rear where he would squat or stand most of the time to work the .30 caliber machine gun on a swivel mount. We fired at long canvas banners towed by another AT-6. [Shortly thereafter, B-17s replaced the trainers as tow ships.] Here we learned actual burst control, how to lead a target and how to judge distance. The pilot would grade us on performance, and our firing accuracy was judged by the number of holes in the target. Our rounds were color coded which identified the gunner firing a particular color.

For our last two weeks of gunnery training we flew every day (weather permitting) and had our ground courses as well, both in the classroom and at the various ranges. The most effective range, as I remember, was a circular course which we drove around in a six-by in a simulated turret from which we fired shotguns at clay targets released by remote control devices. This taught us several vitally needed skills, like quickness and the ability to adapt to rapidly changing conditions.

This was our training program. While brief in nature, it was probably the best that was available at the time. Our instructors, while not having any combat experience, were willing to help their students in every way possible. It must be noted that the students were all volunteers. They wanted to learn; their motivation was to be proficient in their duties and get the missions over with. True, we had a few dropouts, mostly from fear of flying or medical problems, but the number who completed training and went on to combat assignments was outstanding.

After completing gunnery school, most of us went on to other schools for short courses lasting four to six weeks. Then we were assigned to various bases where crews were formed and sent off for transition training in the aircraft they were to fly in combat. A few gunners were sent directly to the various combat theaters as replacement personnel.

As America's Air Force grew and with new planes and equipment being developed, combat crews were completing their missions and coming home to instruct the new personnel coming into service in 1944 and 1945. New and more sophisticated systems were being introduced which called for different and better systems of training. But for the very early days of World War II, we were provided with the best training methods and equipment available at the time.

track him extra smoothly so that it called for almost triple coordination between feet, hands, and eyes. I've always been pretty good at aircraft recognition but head-on, with one shooting at you cramped up in a ball turret with your feet numb from the cold... good luck!

"The Sperry ball was difficult to enter or leave. There was a clutch to engage, mostly by feel. Maybe, in time, one got good at that, but if it wasn't properly engaged, the turret could rotate out from under you when you went to put a leg into it upon entering. It was also mounted in such a manner that a good flak hit on the ship could break it loose. In this event, down you would go, a human bomb! It was uncomfortable operating on the ground in warm weather for just a fifteen minute tracking practice period.

The Sperry ball turret was notoriously small and cramped, uninviting to the unfortunate gunner assigned this unattractive position on our World War II B-17s and B-24s. Small men were chosen for the job. Smithsonian Institution

"The upper turret was best," McDowell maintains. "It probably gave you a false sense of security because very little of your head protruded above the fuselage and it was surrounded by turret metal, plexiglass, and the guns and mounts. Power was transmitted via an electrified collector ring allowing 360 degrees of rotation with no restrictions on how many turns you could make in one direction. Get dizzy, spin forever, or go around only fifteen degrees, whichever you elected. You could also elevate almost ninety degrees so you had a large field of fire and your vision was unrestricted in that field. A fire cutoff cam (interrupter) prevented you from shooting off your own tail. It was probably the easiest turret to get out of in a hurry, and you didn't need anyone to help unless you were wounded.

"The Consolidated tail turret was cramped. It was also difficult to enter and exit and should it jam in either direction, one of the double entry doors couldn't be opened. In that case, in order to get out, you really had a big problem. You had a fair cone of fire from the Consolidated and the visibility was excellent.

"The Emerson nose turret was much the same as the Consolidated tail turret, although a much better

The Sperry ball turret, mounted on a truck bed, was one of the realistic training devices used in flexible gunnery schools. Unlike the Martin upper, with plexiglass cover removed, the Sperry by design had to remain enclosed, a most uncomfortable confinement for student gunners in the heat of the summer. Smithsonian Institution

turret, in my opinion. However, I didn't get to fire either in the air, just those mounted on trucks on the ground. If a hydraulic hose or connection broke on either, you could get a fast fluid bath, depending on pressure, the location of the leak and the size of the break.

"In the early versions of both the B-17 and B-24, the bombardier simply fired a hand-held gun. I always felt perhaps one of fifty gunners could hit the inside of a barn firing from the center with a hand-held. I suppose, in combat, a lot of lucky guys got credit when some unlucky enemy fighter pressed home his attack and flew right into a cone of .50 caliber bullets, aimed in his general direction by some trigger-happy waist gunner who always seemed to have and use more ammo than the boys in the turrets."

Problems in turret training continued to plague the planners. In early 1944, a report by the Military Intelligence Division of the War Department general staff indicated serious deficiencies in the skills of turret gunners sent to the European theater. Some gunners, it was pointed out, were afraid to enter the turret and others didn't know what to do after they did. This required further extensive training by the combat units. Training Command was at a loss to explain the difficulties; they insisted that phase checks—two at flexible gunnery schools, two in the operational training units (OTUs), and two in the combat theaters—were being religiously enforced. Turrets, because of their mechanical complexity, remained a sore spot in flexible gunnery training throughout World War II.

A new day in the morning 6

There must be a better way! This thought dominated every conference and planning session, prompted and encouraged by continuing reports of less than satisfactory results of gunners in combat. Programs changed, new devices and methods were developed, but up until the last months of the war, combat defensive gunnery remained a nagging problem that just wouldn't disappear.

The official *Flexible Gunnery Training in the AAF*, prepared by the Assistant Chief of Staff, Intelligence, Historical Division, contains a chapter on the continuity and control of training. In the leading paragraph it reads: "The graduate of a flexible gunnery school had learned much that was theoretical and much that was practical. Indeed, the task which it was hoped he would complete, first within five weeks and then within six, was so complex and exacting as to make the term 'learned' a relative one. If, as has been said, 'we learn by doing,' the question may arise as to how often and how carefully it is necessary to perform actions before the learning process is satisfactory. Flexible gunnery training was, to some extent, experimental in nature and often gave rise to differences of opinion as to the wisest policies to follow. Inquiry, discussion, and the willingness to profit by the lessons of experience were fundamental factors in the steady improvement manifested in the training program as time went on."

It was apparent almost from the moment we went to war that gunnery students were not retaining the skills they supposedly had mastered. As early as 1942, Kingman requested appropriate training equipment and devices for OTUs in order to pursue refresher training in flexible gunnery. This was proposed as a means of solving the demonstrated problem of poor learning retention by school graduates. A special board of officers formed to study the problem determined that this poor retention could be attributed to three things: lack of equipment; utilization of equipment with which students were unfamiliar; and loss of time moving from one station to another. The board suggested that control of replacement training by the Flying Training Command would provide the best solution. It was natural, therefore, to direct continuity of training to the various air forces, as a follow-up to the sketchy nature and brief period of the course of instruction in the various schools.

Misgivings about the effectiveness of gunnery training extended all the way up to the highest echelons. General H. H. (Hap) Arnold, the Air Force big boss, complained in a letter to Training Command that "reports are still being received which indicate a serious lack of gunnery training for our aerial gunners . . ." Planners and instructors were trying, as attested by the ongoing changes in curricula and procedures, but the frustrations continued to mount and combat personnel still did not live up to expectations.

In 1943 the Director of Bombardment at Headquarters AAF also called attention to the lack of proficiency on the part of combat gunners. The OTUs insisted they had a standard, effective program of gunnery training, but had been hampered by a lack of equipment. The most serious deficiencies in this regard involved tools, spare parts and tow-target aircraft. The OTUs further maintained that each gunner was provided turret manipulation instruction consisting of four hours a day for four weeks, in addition to five high altitude missions during which each gunner was instructed in the use of oxygen equipment. Gunners were also required to fire their guns on each mission, it was maintained, and this enabled them to become familiar with those malfunctions which might occur due to the freezing conditions encountered at high altitude. However, no gun cameras were used at that time because they were not available. The OTUs also claimed that much theoretical training had been abandoned in favor of more practical methods.

One result of all this turmoil prompted a report from the air staff recommending that gunnery instruction be standardized, both in the Training Command and the air forces. It also suggested that Training Command be prohibited from graduating and shipping personnel to the air forces until students had reached an acceptable level of proficiency.

In the fall of 1943, Training Command received queries from AAF regarding deficiencies turned up by subsequent phase checks. Training Command, in its reply, insisted the primary reason for the apparent lack of graduate proficiency was the length of time, as much as nine months in some instances, between the completion of training and arrival at OTUs and RTUs (replacement training units). This prompted air staff to recommend steps to expedite the flow of students to assuming commands, hoping, no doubt, to lay the matter to rest once and for all.

Ineffective as it appeared to some, the outcome gave added emphasis in 1944 to phase checks, standardization and closer liaison between training agencies. Seeking a practical means of testing student abilities, phase checking was considered particularly important, and before the end of 1943, Training Command had made it clear that phase checks were intended, not only to identify student deficiencies but also to correct those existing deficiencies. The final result was the introduction in February of 1944 of standard phase check forms to all flexible gunnery installations. This was designed to ensure a uniform standard of evaluating the skill levels of all school graduates.

Through all the growing pains of building an effective training program, the nagging thought persisted that something was lacking. Indeed there was, and through the efforts of a few dedicated and farseeing individuals, an entirely new concept, employing all of the basic tenets of the learning process, began to emerge. To those directly involved, the main disappointment of the entire flexible gunnery training program was that it hadn't begun earlier. As it was, the frangible bullet phase did not start until the outcome of the war had already been pretty well decided. It was canceled before it could be properly developed but it proved to be an exciting and controversial training device. It deserved more credit than it received.

One man deserves the credit for starting it all. The synthetic training aids officer at Harlingen in the spring of 1942, Major Cameron D. Fairchild, knew there must be a better way to train gunners for combat. Viewing the current training methods, like shooting skeet from moving vehicles, utilizing synthetic devices and firing at aerial cloth targets, Fairchild visualized a system where the student would be placed in a realistic mock combat situation, firing live ammunition at an aircraft making simulated attacks on a bomber. Fairchild felt that this would provide the only truly effective training. It would negate the objections of psychologists monitoring the school programs who were convinced that ". . . air-to-air firing as now conducted is, for most students, a bewildering emotional experience which quite effectively smothers learning."

Labeled by some a lesser Billy Mitchell, Fairchild was only a major in the Army Air Forces Reserve and far down the administrative and operational chains of command. He was zealous to a fault and so dedicated to his radical concept that he risked rebuke—and worse—to see that his proposals received proper attention. Defying the tradition of ordnance development, Fairchild and two converts, Paul Gross and Marcus Hobbs of Duke University, embarked on a three-year struggle which eventually resulted in the frangible bullet program.

In the beginning, Fairchild was convinced that the only drawback to the simulation he had in mind was the development of a machine gun bullet that could strike a target aircraft without damaging the plane or its pilot. Despite the absence of any kind of encouragement, Fairchild pursued his idea by writing to more than 100 colleges and universities asking for assistance. Most of the responses were completely negative, classifying his proposal as just another crackpot scheme. Of the eighty replies received, two proved important to the eventual success of the concept he was zealously promoting.

At Duke University, Fairchild's letter was referred to Professor Paul Gross, director of research at this eminent southern institution. Further correspondence convinced Gross that the plan had merit, and he made a personal visit, at his own expense, to Harlingen. There he was treated to a three-day examination of current training methods and, from personal participation, concluded (as had Fairchild) that these methods were entirely at variance with the product they were designed to produce. He became an enthusiastic convert to Fairchild's "brainstorm" and was convinced from the start that a new bullet, harmless to properly protected airplanes, could be developed.

Concurrent with Gross' entry into the flexible gunnery training dichotomy, Professor A. D. Moore of Michigan University's engineering school, came forward with the suggestion of developing a bullet of tempered glass, somewhat like the Prince Rupert's drop. (A Prince Rupert's drop is formed by dropping molten glass into cold water. The resultant gourd-shaped drop is under mechanical stress such that when the neck is fractured, failure occurs throughout the entire drop, simulating a miniature explosion.) Moore contacted Gross who saw possibilities in the glass bullet and, although the project eventually took an entirely different form, the drops remained a strong selling point in future discussions with high-level military chiefs.

Gross contacted Marcus E. Hobbs, assistant professor of physical chemistry at Duke, who immediately expressed interest in the novel proposal. Hobbs, like Gross, remained a faithful collaborator to the end of the project. Together, the two professors conducted many experiments on a gunnery range, firing both glass and bakelite (phenolic resin, one of the early plastics) projectiles from .22 caliber rifles. All of the bullets shattered on impact with light sheet metal, and although the decreased velocities could only be approximated at this time, test results proved encouraging.

By July, Fairchild had finally obtained permission from intermediate levels of command to take his concept to the National Defense Research Committee (NDRC). He contacted Gross and told him he wanted to visit glass companies, indicating he was impressed with the tests Gross had conducted. Gross replied to Fairchild that phenolic resins showed as much or more promise than glass. On July 15, 1942, Fairchild, accompanied by Gross, called on R. C. Tolman, vice chairman of NDRC, who summoned other representatives to consider this obviously "impossible" task of firing a projectile from a standard machine gun at an "attacking" airplane without damaging the target or its pilot. Despite the immensity of the concept, subsequent conferences in July and August (the first at Princeton University), produced some guidelines promising possible solutions, and terms of cooperation between the various working bodies were agreed upon.

It was stipulated that Duke would continue, on its own, to experiment with various materials for the bullet. Gross and his fellow academicians would be assisted by the Bakelite Corporation participating on a voluntary basis. Princeton would conduct trial firings and assist Duke in making velocity-measuring devices. NDRC personnel would be responsible for making necessary calculations to modify an optical gunsight. The modification would be necessary for the sight to compensate for the anticipated changes in the projectile's ballistic characteristics. In addition, all assistance would be provided Fairchild to obtain an official contract for NDRC which would enable that body to write subcontracts with Duke and any others who might possibly contribute to the project. It was pointed out that development of this training system would require the extensive use of facilities available to NDRC through military support. This was important: NDRC owned no aircraft.

It was immediately apparent that the project involved two major army departments, Ordnance and the Air Force. An objection or refusal by either to consider frangible bullets could doom any effort on the part of NDRC, negating time spent on research. In addition, the NDRC division assigned to the frangible bullet project had to balance this against other demands, some of which showed more promise than the one to which Fairchild and Gross were dedicated. Young men employed by NDRC were mostly draft eligible, and Selective Service regulations permitted their deferment only when actively engaged in official support projects. It should be noted that official support was difficult to obtain for those programs requiring long-term research. Had these real and assumed barriers been absent, the frangible bullet project would certainly have progressed much faster.

At any rate, a high-level conference was scheduled in September at the Pentagon where Fairchild and Gross presented their training concept to representatives of the Army Air Forces, the Army Ordnance Department, and the navy, with NDRC appearing in the role of interested party. The representatives concurred immediately on the desirability of the proposal, and the discussion continued at great length. It soon became apparent that this radical concept posed unforeseen problems not easy to solve. Among the separate topics discussed were the type and composition of the frangible bullet, what kind and how much armor the "attacking" aircraft would have to carry, and to what extent the standard velocity of the projectile would have to be lowered in the interest of safety. They decided that the participating aircraft speeds would have to be decreased and, in order to keep the student gunner's sight picture unchanged, the optical gunsight would require modification to compensate for the speed changes.

Finally, they covered the development of a system of scoring hits on the target, recognizing that an entirely new concept was involved, invalidating all of the traditional methods still in use with current firing practices. With broad guidelines provided by the working members of the conference, Professor Gross headed back to Duke University to begin work on the frangible bullet. Fairchild returned to Harlingen to start developing a suitable target airplane.

The conference did not, by any means, produce unanimity among the various members. Ordnance, especially, proved a thorn in the side of harmony and while they came up with some definitive objections and practical solutions, the feeling they generated among conference colleagues was mostly one of exasperation. Although Ordnance did not press their objections at this time, they suggested that the frangible bullet might break and jam in the machine guns (this did in fact occur on a number of occasions when the program got under way and posed some vexing problems before it was solved); the ballistics might not match the service projectile closely enough to provide realistic training; and protective armor on the target aircraft might prove too heavy, seriously inhibiting its performance.

In the days ahead, these points were to be resurrected many times by this seemingly recalcitrant service branch. In addition, Ordnance contended that NDRC was not needed, that Ordnance could develop the bullet without outside help, provided Air Force would make the request specific. Finally, it was agreed that Air Force would submit a request for Ordnance to set up a project for the bullet and gun, and provide initial specifications for feasible armor the target plane could be expected to carry. Ordnance would request assistance from NDRC if needed, and the conference concluded on a note of high hope. Some attendees, writing for various technical journals, waxed downright euphoric in their enthusiastic evaluation of the work accomplished.

Fairchild and Gross went at their assigned tasks with energy and enthusiasm, anticipating smooth sailing ahead and expecting a successful conclusion to their dream. Duke and Bakelite continued to work gratis, with Princeton also participating. Soon, however, a problem arose which resulted in a serious extended delay to the entire program. It seems that Air Force sent Ordnance a project request including only the requirement for bullet development, without mentioning the rest of the items the conference had identified. Ordnance, therefore, refused to grant official status and, intimating that the Air Force member of the Ordnance planning committee was opposed to the project (interpreting this as dissension within the AAF), insisted that this discrepancy be addressed first.

NDRC was in a quandary. Considerable progress had already been made and those on the working committee took no pleasure at the prospect of discontinuing the project. In the meantime, however, it was deemed necessary to notify Princeton to halt its work and NDRC decided to issue a formal progress report. It was hoped this action would bestir the military officials sufficiently to get the frangible bullet program off top dead center. Meanwhile, informal cooperation between the participating parties continued. They made specific computations at this time (adding to those already produced by Princeton) on scaling or reducing weapon range, together with the attendant compensation of sights. This marked a definite breakthrough in providing realistic muzzle velocities.

The whole project was really saved by the tenacious efforts of Duke University and the Bakelite Corporation. Bakelite proceeded with their production of bullets of various compositions, and Duke continued to experiment with them, assisted now by the volunteer efforts of Dr. Katherine Jeffers of the university's

Department of Zoology. Fairchild and Gross, meanwhile, continued vigorously to press for official support, resulting in a letter on December 1, 1942, to the AAF director of military requirements. The letter, originated by Gross, outlined the situation and expressed his faith in the project and his concern at the apparent lack of progress. Air Force replied immediately. Their courteously negative response said, in part:

"This office did initiate a project through the Ordnance Department which has as its object the development of a type of projectile which could be fired from standard aircraft machine guns against target airplanes for use in aircraft gunnery training. It was necessary that the target airplane be a normal airplane unarmored. [Why this reference to an unarmored target plane is not clear. Of course the final product was armored, as stipulated in the earliest considerations.] Although the project did not clearly appear to be possible of successful completion, nevertheless the value of such a projectile was so great, the interest of Captain (sic) Fairchild was so intense and the progress at that time had been so far above expectations, this office did believe that further study and investigation were warranted. The Ordnance Department, basing their opinion on experience and background in that department, held little hope for its success and were not particularly enthusiastic about continuing the investigation. Only recently the Ordnance Department indicated that a target airplane would require armor in thickness from 3/16 to ¼ inch and possibly a little thicker. Such a requirement, of course, definitely precluded any further consideration of the project, the Ordnance Department being so advised."

The conclusion of the letter offered an out. If the armor conclusions were proven incorrect, AAF said, the project could be revived. This gave Gross an opening and he fired right back. He pointed out that legitimate experiments and calculations to date showed, irrefutably, that armor thickness of more than ⅛ inch steel would not be required. He also said he was confident aluminum alloy could be used without adversely affecting safety to target or pilot.

Gross's letter brought the engineering section of Materiel Command into the act. They, too, followed the doubters' line, insisting that Gross's calculations were in error and those of Ordnance correct. They added that the director of military requirements still insisted on an unarmored target aircraft. They further stated that Ordnance disputed the experimental calculations on bullet trajectory and gun muzzle velocity. All of these factors, they claimed, combined to disapprove official status for the project.

Gross at last became disheartened, and he could hardly be blamed. During the ongoing arguments between Gross and the military, Fairchild was kept fully informed. They temporarily gave up hope of obtaining a formal project, but they persevered nonetheless. Fairchild managed to obtain some support from his commander, Colonel William Kennedy (the same officer who had traveled with the fact-finding team to England) and this, more than any other factor, kept the dream alive. Defying the considerable array of official opinion, Kennedy continued to issue orders permitting Fairchild to travel extensively. On these monthly trips, Fairchild managed to visit Duke University, Bakelite Corporation, Princeton University and the Corning Glass Works. Contacts continued with Corning until 1943 when it became obvious that the plastic-metal bullet composition was the better of the two.

The first mold for producing the bakelite blanks was ordered and paid for in the spring of 1943 from funds provided by Flying Training Command. This was at the instigation of Fairchild, who appeared to be all things to all men at this critical time, and who managed to keep his activities more or less hidden from the disapproving eyes of Ordnance and Materiel Command. The mold greatly expedited the production of frangible bullets which, up to this time, had been handmade. To its everlasting credit, Flying Training Command had faith in the concept and, in the summer of 1943, assigned three men as Fairchild's assistants, Lieutenant Paul Greig, Lieutenant Homer Henderson and Corporal Jenneman.

These men proved invaluable to the project. Greig was an Ordnance officer (assigned to Training Command) and remained with the program until reassigned late in 1944. Henderson succeeded Fairchild in the program's later stages and became the key man in the continuing project. He was promoted to major prior to his discharge in September of 1945. Jenneman was a valuable assistant who willingly accepted and performed well in various capacities. He, too, was a staunch supporter of the frangible bullet as a training tool.

By late summer of 1943 it had become clear that lead-filled bakelite bullets, of proper density, could be produced with sufficient frangibility to satisfy the stringent requirements of the program. Participating members of DuPont were making progress in selecting the proper powder for the final round. At the same time, testing was being concluded on various types and thicknesses of armor for the target airplane, indicating that Flying Training Command was forging ahead, despite the baleful warnings of other commands. It should be borne in mind that there was no violation of orders here; Headquarters AAF had not *prohibited* the continuing development of the frangible bullet. It had merely passed on comments and evaluations of parallel and subordinate commands.

Meanwhile, NDRC was lying low, waiting for and anticipating evidence from the combat theaters on the need for better gunnery training. This was forthcoming in a report by a Headquarters AAF investigating officer on a survey tour of the Mediterranean area. NDRC immediately returned to the attack. The result was a conference by NDRC personnel, chaired by Dr. J. B. Conant, which reiterated NDRC's acceptance of the frangible bullet approach. Out of this came a special committee assigned the task of recommending a spe-

Graphic demonstration of the manner in which the T-44 frangible bullet crumbled on impact. Pinball pilots found that even pieces of a frangible projectile could cause aircraft damage to vulnerable parts. US Air Force

cific program for obtaining military service support. The committee was enjoined to foresee and answer all possible objections to the project. It was obvious that NDRC wanted it to live and was prepared to do everything in its power to ensure success. A report was submitted December 1, 1943 and conversations with the Air Force were quickly initiated.

Other pressures were developing within the military services. Engineers tested proposed types of armor at Wright Field and they appeared promising.

Frangible ammunition in original container. Single round stands on top. Frangible ammunition, identified as T-44, carried a green band around the nose of the bullet to distinguish it from regular .30 caliber rounds. Author's collection

Studying all the test results and heeding the persuasive recommendations of NDRC, damage trials of an armored A-20 wing section were requested. The tests were made with satisfactory results and, at long last, NDRC managed to obtain acceptance of the project.

Subsequently, Gross got together with key NDRC personnel and obtained a formal contract for Duke University. This permitted Duke to press forward in its substantial contribution, with outside funds. It also gave rise to an increase in working personnel at the university and the issuance of a subcontract to the Bakelite Corporation in April of 1944. Bakelite immediately began producing experimental bullets while Duke continued its work under Gross and Hobbs with an augmented staff. Duke modified the .30 caliber Browning machine gun by installing a gas-operated piston booster at the muzzle. This permitted operation of the weapon with the lighter powder charge carried by the frangible ammunition, adding just enough boost to the barrel's recoil momentum to make the gun operate properly. Two of these guns were installed in the Martin turret of a modified B-17 and tested on the ground, using 1,500 rounds of ammunition made from Bakelite molds and hand-loaded at Duke.

The final task of the project involved the development of a device for detecting and scoring hits on the

This is the counter designed to keep track of hits on the RP-63. This is a view of the cockpit of the "A" model. In the RP-63C, the counter was relocated to the floor on the right-hand side of the pilot's seat. Here a Laredo pinball pilot points to the counter. Note the padded gunsight. Pilots learned to use the sight to make proper curves of pursuit. US Air Force

target aircraft. Sperry Gyroscope Company of Brooklyn, New York, came up with an ingenious solution. It involved the development of a device designed around a type of microphone, a radiosonic gadget of the kind previously used to detect detonation in internal combustion engines. Attached to the inside of the target plane's armor, these sensors would pick up vibrations made by the impact of an object. This, in turn, would induce an electric current which, properly amplified, would trigger a counter device in the target aircraft's cockpit. Simultaneous with activation of the counter, an external red light mounted in the opening of the propeller spinner where the 20 mm cannon used to protrude would flash. The cockpit counter, backup for the flashing light which the student gunner could see, would enable the target pilot to count and make a record of hits.

As sophisticated and promising as it appeared in the beginning, the system resulted eventually in uncovering the most significant problems of the frangible bullet program. This was not apparent at the final testing stage, however, and planners were convinced that the project was at long last off the ground. All previous exasperations faded in view of the anticipated success of what proved to be the most innovative training concept ever conceived and put into effect. The question remained: *Would it work?* The answer was forthcoming.

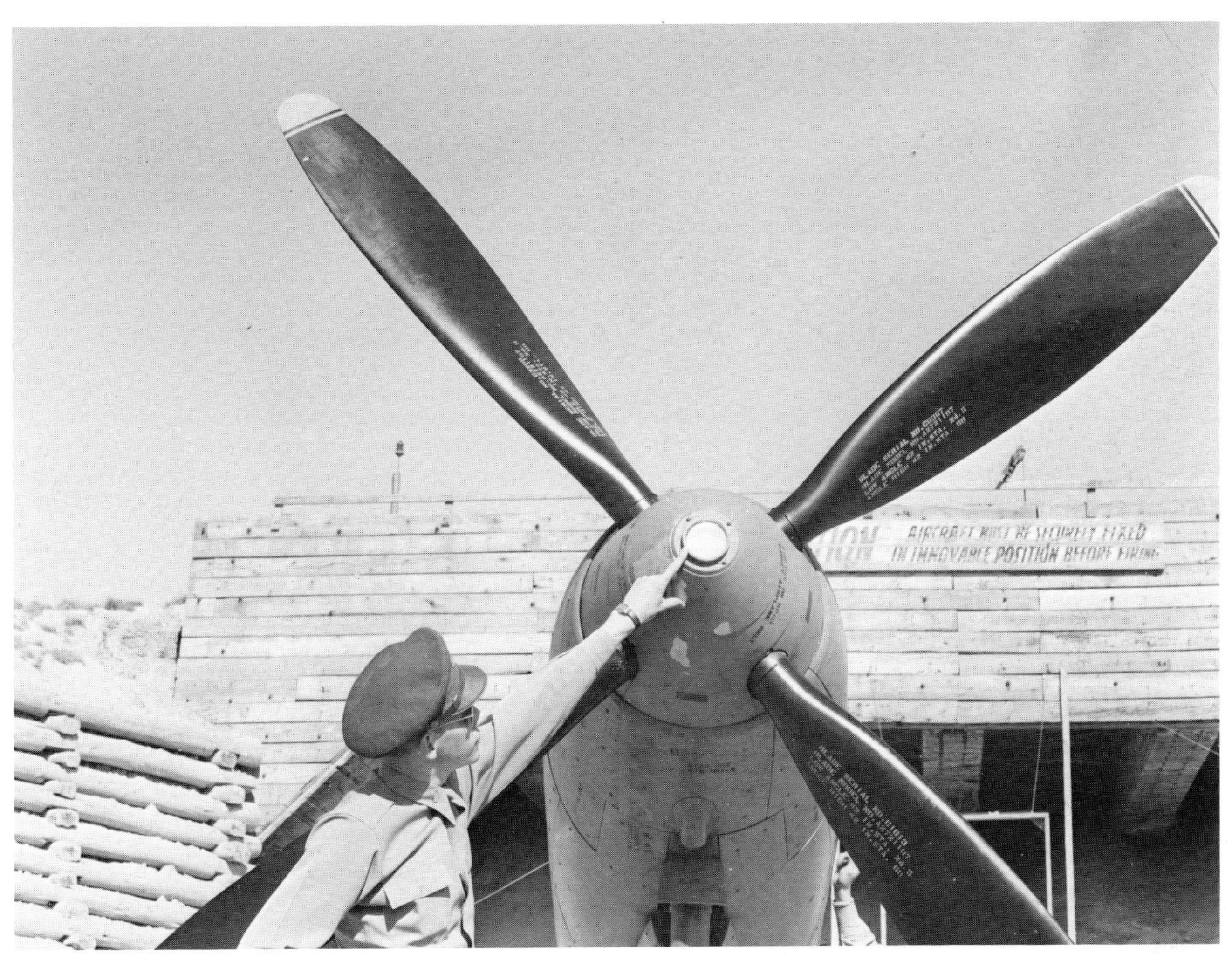

This is the location of the red light which was supposed to indicate hits to student gunners. It was not very effective. Few undergoing frangible bullet training can recall ever seeing the light flash. This configuration was typical of the RP-63As and Cs. Multiple lights were installed on wingtips and fuselage of the "G" model. US Air Force

We're airborne! 7

Major Fairchild utilized the intervening period to good advantage. In addition to collaborating with Gross on the overall supervision of the fledgling project, he worked on the development of a suitable target aircraft. His initial efforts almost ended in disaster, as we shall see later, involving the airplane he chose for the first tests. The Bell P-63, which eventually proved so well-suited for the task, did not even rate consideration in the beginning. Fairchild chose the twin-engined A-20, a high-performance, combat-proven attack and light bomber for the target at first, and persuaded the Aircraft Laboratory of the Air Technical Service Command at Wright Field to convert one for frangible bullet tests. The laboratory covered the aircraft with lightweight duralumin armor, and early in 1944 an armored A-20 wing section withstood test firing as described in the preceding chapter.

The initial field trials began on May 29, 1944, when all system components were brought together at Buckingham Field. Two A-20 pilots with extensive combat experience in the Pacific Theater, Captains Charles T. Everett and J. B. Roan, were ordered to the Florida base to become the first to fly a frangible bullet target airplane, this one nicknamed "Alclad Nag." Their orders indicated only that they were to try out a new kind of ammunition on a volunteer basis. There was no mention in their orders that they would actually be fired upon. They assumed they would be on the other firing end and when they learned the true circumstances of the program and what part they would play in the tests, they were plainly perturbed. This was particularly true of Everett who, as Fairchild later remarked, ". . . was the maddest captain I ever saw!"

In order to allay the fears of the target pilots, Fairchild, Gross and Joseph Evans of Wright Field each took turns in the cockpit of *Alclad Nag* while frangible ammunition was fired at them from a distance of about twenty-five yards. Convinced the target plane wasn't that bad after all and mollified to an extent, the two pilots agreed to participate in the flying test phase. The selection of these two individuals was most fortunate; they proved especially skillful in handling the overweight A-20, no mean feat as it turned out.

The first air-to-air trials were conducted with Everett at the controls of the A-20. Several runs were made employing the classic curve of pursuit, with Sergeant Karp in the forward upper turret of a YB-40 (a converted B-17F with multiple guns, designed to be used as a defensive escort for bomber formations) and Sergeant Oldham calling range from the upper rear turret. Hits were made and they were registered by the cockpit counter of the A-20. Hopes rose when a number of successful missions were flown that first day.

The second day, with things seemingly going well, catastrophe threatened. One engine of *Alclad Nag* quit and the heavy aircraft, unable to fly properly with only

The original Pinball. *Lt. Col. Donald B. Russell selected the P-63 as the frangible gunnery target aircraft mainly because it was available for training without degrading our combat efforts, and because it bore a close head-on resemblance to the German Bf 109. Russell personally assisted in renovating the first two '63s. The other aircraft was named* Frangible Sal. Smithsonian Institution

one "fan" operating, rapidly lost altitude. Everett was the pilot on this mission and he displayed exceptional skill in the emergency. He calmly reported his difficulty and headed for the nearest auxiliary field some twenty miles distant. Observers and various officials at the site were engaging in collective heart attacks by this time, but Everett made the auxiliary field and landed without further incident. Everett had saved a valuable machine and gave accident investigators an intact aircraft to examine.

Without doubt, the frangible bullet project would have come to an inglorious end right there if the experimental aircraft had crashed and the engine failure had been found to be caused by a frangible bullet. However, a mechanical defect was determined to be the culprit and, undaunted, the two test pilots continued their flights after the A-20's defective engine was replaced. The tests were completed without further incident and results were considered so satisfactory, the project was approved for inclusion in the formal flexible gunnery training program. Fairchild and Gross worked closely with Flying Training Command top officials in spelling out modifications to flexible gunnery plans, and everyone began gearing up for this exciting new concept.

As successful as the air-to-air firing tests had been, it became apparent from the first that the A-20 was not the best target aircraft available. Conferences were held to determine a final choice which, it was decided, should be similar in size and performance to the Messerschmitt Bf 109, then being used in large numbers by the Germans in Europe. The final selection was left to Lieutenant Colonel Donald S. Russell of Laredo Army Airfield.

Russell began visiting the plants manufacturing fighter-type aircraft, and reported his findings and recommendations to Brigadier General E. B. Lyon, Training Command's deputy for flexible gunnery. The ultimate selection of Bell Aircraft's P-63 Kingcobra came as no real surprise, everything considered.

A refinement of the earlier engine-behind-the-pilot P-39 Airacobra, this unique fighter was a superior performer. Originally designed as a competitor of the P-51 and P-47, two airplanes performing yeoman wartime service for the Air Force in all theaters, the P-63 had been ignored by the United States for combat duty. It was in production mainly because the United States supplied it in large numbers to the Russians who loved both the P-39 and P-63 and utilized them with excellent effect, mostly in ground support roles.

The P-63 was readily available for training purposes, which suited the frangible bullet planners to a "T." It was first used by Flying Training Command on gun camera missions and had already made a favorable impression on the pilots privileged to fly it. The selection of this aircraft brought the Bell Aircraft Company

Pinballs "attacking" the YB-40 Pea Shooter *at Laredo during shakedown missions of the frangible bullet training program. Two are in curve of pursuit with two more waiting in the distance. The regular pinball missions were conducted with one fighter against one bomber.* Smithsonian Institution

into the development phase of the frangible bullet target, and the energy and dedication of Bell personnel gave important impetus to the program.

Planners had previously stipulated that the target airplane would be armored against all head-on firing within thirty degrees of the plane's line of flight. They assumed that the curve of pursuit would be employed on all passes against the firing aircraft, thus negating the need for extending the armor over any part of the plane not normally struck by bullets. They also assumed that gunners would cease firing at the proper angle-off. This assumption proved false in subsequent training missions, and although the incidence of such deviations from plan was minimal, some target aircraft did come to grief from students firing on the break. The armored version of the chosen fighter was designated RP-63, the "R" standing for "Restricted From Combat."

Russell arrived at Bell's Niagara, New York, plant on July 19, 1944, to supervise construction of the first five RP-63 aircraft. The building phase presented some unforeseen difficulties, occasioned mainly by an entirely new building process. Armor plates, up to ¼ inch thick, had to be shaped to the airplane's contours and bolted to the original skin. What originally appeared to be a simple procedure turned out to be extremely complicated. The thicker duralumin plates tended to break the drop hammer dies used in forming the thinner material from which the P-63 was constructed. As Col. Russell described it: "In practically every instance on the first three airplanes it was necessary to shape each piece (of armor) by hand and rollers. In Department 86, we set up solid steel tables and secured them with fifty-pound sacks of sand. The steel tables, with sand sacks, an eight-pound sledge, plenty of sweat, and a desire to build this airplane shaped these pieces . . . Two of those ships, *Pinball* and *Frangible Sal,* are the two airplanes I built . . ."

Russell and the Bell people persevered. The hand-built prototypes flew in August of 1944, a remarkable achievement considering the date work actually began. Bell Aircraft was now awarded the contract to manufacture another 95 RP-63As, and production began immediately. At the same time, studies were made to improve the hit-registering pickup system on the airplanes. Three separate and seemingly effective systems were worked out by Duke University, Sperry and Bell Aircraft. Bell produced an amplifier superior to the others, and it was adopted for installation in the remaining RPs. By this time the first target airplanes had arrived at Laredo and right away the project began to be referred to as "Pinball," derived, of course, from the nickname of one of the first prototypes.

By the time the target airplanes were ready, Duke University had the frangible bullet ammunition fully developed and available in quantity. Ordnance Department approved the design, grudgingly no doubt, on August 31, 1944. It identified the new ammunition in military jargon as "Cartridge, Ball, Frangible, Caliber .30, T-44." The green bullet tip, followed by a white band, distinguished it from other .30 caliber ammunition with their own color codes. This important factor was intended to prevent the insertion of higher powered bullets which would, undoubtedly, have caused safety problems of monumental proportions. Laredo was the first base to receive frangible ammunition, the first shipment arriving in December of 1944.

Laredo also initiated the first pinball training missions and here most of the early bugs were eliminated. (Hereafter, the term "pinball" will be used interchangeably with "frangible bullet" in describing the new program.) T-9 machine guns (those weapons specially adapted for use with frangible ammunition) were installed in three different bombers (B-17, B-24 and B-29) and the first tentative missions were flown. To compensate for the decreased muzzle velocities, it had been determined that aircraft speeds would have to be reduced approximately thirty percent. Consequently, the Sperry K-13 compensating sight was modified to correspond to the reduced aircraft speeds, while another sight was being developed specifically for frangible missions. Aberdeen Proving Grounds prepared range tables, based on their ballistic determinations, for use by sight manufacturers in modifying their devices. This was completed in the fall of 1944 but little actual work was done on sight modification until early 1945. Working with Duke University personnel, Capt. Henderson modified the sights used successfully by the first training classes.

Colonel E. M. Day became commander of Laredo Army Airfield late in 1944. Under his aegis the pinball missions quickly became the focal point of flexible gunnery training. He was instrumental in installing cameras alongside T-9 machine guns. This allowed instructors, during postflight critiques, to evaluate students' target-tracking ability, but it didn't work very well. It was found that the vibration of the gun pretty well destroyed the integrity of the cameras and they remained mostly ineffective as training evaluators until Kingman came up with a workable mount.

In March of 1945 the Air Force gave a public demonstration of the new program. This marked Major Fairchild's last important contribution to the pinball project. He was beset with a nagging illness which, together with his regular duties, kept him away much of the time from the program to which he had devoted so much time and effort. Discharged from the Army in May, he was awarded the well-deserved Legion of Merit. Many people maintain this belated recognition was small recompense for his many contributions and sacrifices.

In April of 1945 all seven flexible gunnery schools were well into the frangible bullet missions. By this time, the initial fleet of 100 RP-63A airplanes—they were distributed almost equally among the training bases—had been augmented by 200 RP-63Cs, a later version equipped with another model Allison engine. The pinball exercises generated considerable interest and enthusiasm among interested parties, although the reception from some of the target pilots could only be characterized as lukewarm. Las Vegas hosted a conference of gunnery experts shortly after frangible firing began. It concluded that the recently installed program was "the most successful and best training device developed to date." General Lyon, recognizing the superior and unique quality of the frangible bullet effort and the contribution of the originator, congratulated Major Fairchild just before his discharge. He wrote: "It is the development which will revolutionize gunnery training."

Perhaps no program was ever rushed into being as quickly as the pinball, considering that less than a year elapsed from the first air-to-air firing tests until the system was officially installed in the gunnery schools. This was ironic indeed in view of the obstacles initially presented by recalcitrant entities, and probably had much to do with this alacrity. However, the speed with which the fledgling program was implemented prevented the identification and elimination of numerous flaws uncovered as time went on.

It became immediately apparent that frangible ammunition, which had performed so admirably during static and airborne tests, would have to be modified to do the job. The bullets displayed a disconcerting tendency to break off at the tips in heavy training usage, causing the machine guns to jam. These "short rounds" continued to plague the project and although a short round eliminator was devised to alleviate the problem, it was never completely solved. Progress was made after many modifications, but jamming, on a lesser scale, continued to exasperate officials right up to the end of the program.

Other problems cropped up. It was found that the powder used in the ammunition was not burning cleanly, causing accumulated carbon deposits and further jamming. This necessitated the modification of the piston booster adapter. In addition, it was well-nigh impossible to adjust the hit indicator devices on the target airplanes, and this resulted in frequent false readings. The trouble stemmed from sensitivity adjustments. If too sensitive, target pilots will attest, the cockpit counter would spin like crazy on just the slightest hint of a rough landing. Conversely, if the adjustments were made too insensitive, the indicators would not work at all. The development of dependable hit indicators lagged far behind all other phases of the pinball program and provided the single most serious objection to the system from the gunner's point of view.

Prone to lose its adjustment during periods of prolonged firing, the K-13 gunsight gave its share of trouble. Together with all of the other difficulties, this contributed to a disappointingly low percentage of recorded hits—less than one percent on many training missions. With all these distractions and problems, however, the system had proven invaluable as an aid to the gunnery training process, and gunners will tell you it gave the most realistic means of preparing them for the combat environment.

Target aircraft came in for a share of the blame. The RP-63, like the preceding Bell fighters, was powered by the liquid-cooled Allison engine and, like the P-39 and P-63, carried oil and coolant radiators beneath the fuselage in both wing roots. Cooling air was directed to them through ducts with openings inboard at the wing's leading edge. The ducts on the RPs were protected by curved louvers, designed to cause an entering frangible bullet to disintegrate, thus protecting the delicate radiator membranes. Not all of the frangible projectiles behaved as they should, however, and numerous forced landings resulted from the loss of coolant or lubricating oil.

Target aircraft also became disabled through no fault of the airplane's design. Firing on the break was strictly forbidden but, as we all know, laws and regulations are made to be broken. The RP was required to turn to the same side as the pursuit curve, thus exposing the unarmored belly to any "trigger happy" student obsessed with the prospect of making that "kill." Pilots relate the universally uncomfortable feeling accompanying such transgressions. To glance over one's shoulder on the break—usually the left; most RP passes were made from the bomber's right side—and see smoke issuing from the muzzle of a machine gun, disposed a person to considerable concern and usually resulted in communication of violent nature to the crew of the offending bomber. At any rate, the incidence of forced landings throughout Air Training Command contributed to the grounding of the entire RP-63 fleet in early August of 1945. Five accidents or incidents occurred in one week at Las Vegas alone prior to grounding.

One result of these unfortunate happenings was a modification of the louvers in the wing ducts. At the same time, Bell Aircraft was awarded a contract for 450 RP-63G target planes, a new version with heavier armor, relocated flashing lights and 100 more horsepower. Delivery was scheduled to begin in September, confirming the Air Force's commitment to the pinball and giving promise of an extensive continuation of the project.

Several other improvements to the program were under way. A new type of frangible ammunition, the T-74 cartridge boasting more effective powder, was being tested. This gave promise of providing consistent bullet velocities in addition to leaving fewer carbon deposits. Training Command anticipated this development would drastically curtail piston booster failure, one of the pernicious problems affecting the program from its inception. There were also instances of regular bullets intermingled with frangible ammunition, and while no serious incidents were attributed to these few foul-ups, the implications were enough to give planners some anxious moments. Designs to change the physical shape of the frangible bullet were made but never accepted.

Hal Broxton remembers some of the difficulties posed by frangible bullets. Just returned from combat, Broxton was assigned assistant ordnance supply officer at Kingman. "Part of my duties consisted of certifying that all shell casings were empty before being returned to the factory for reloading," he says. "Since we fired, I believe, over one million rounds of the .30 caliber frangibles each day, there was no way that even fifty supply officers could inspect each shell casing. [Broxton's estimate of the daily ammunition expenditure is way too high, but it detracts very little from the immensity of the inspection task.] Therefore, I certified on the basis of random sampling. The frangibles had a nasty habit sometimes of breaking flush with the casing, which shouldn't have been a problem because it would still fire, supposedly. Hopefully, these would be detected by the armament personnel and segregated for special disposition.

"Needless to say, one of the rounds wound up in a lot which had been certified by me, and exploded at the factory during the reloading process. I'm not aware of the extent of the damages but I sure had a lot of very important visitors."

John L. Gornall was also closely identified with frangible bullet maintenance and supply. He was ordnance supply officer at Tyndall and was responsible for ammo receipt, linking and delivery to the firing aircraft. "I remember we hand-linked the .30 ammunition to avoid clipping the bullets," Gornall relates. "We also had to inspect for regular .30 caliber live ammo, which had a much greater charge of powder. Only one round could get through the specially-configured machine gun because the recoil cylinder would seize and interrupt firing. We knew that one round of regular ammunition could prove fatal to a target aircraft pilot. We discovered several rounds in ammunition we received (I believe) from Rock Island Arsenal in Illinois. This was reported to the FBI, I was told, but I have no knowledge of the result."

The extent of the Air Force commitment to the pinball program is evidenced by the design of a completely new target aircraft still on the drafting boards at the end of World War II. This was the RP-63Z, a much superior version of the Bell fighter with thicker armor built into the structure. It marked a distinct departure from the construction methods employed on previous RPs with armor attached to the original aircraft skin. However, all plans for the improvement of the frangible bullet program fell victim to our rapid demobilization after Japan surrendered and the war was over. None of the projected improvements reached the production stage. Much of Bell's retooling went to scrap; it is not known if the US government assumed any portion of the loss.

Although work continued on all phases of the pinball project well into August of 1945, its days were numbered. On V-J Day, almost 300 of the original RP-63 airplanes were in use in the seven gunnery schools, although actual firing missions had been halted for some time. During the short life of the pinball program, students flew approximately 11,000 pinball training missions in which some 13,000,000 rounds of ammunition were expended. In August of 1945, the scheduled production of frangible ammo was set at 45,000,000 rounds per month. Ironically, just before V-J Day a statement emanated from Headquarters AAF to the effect that "all firing from the air in the gunnery training program will be with frangible bullets."

So this innovative program came to an end. A concept that promised so much fell victim to the euphoria accompanying the end of hostilities, and RP-63G procurement was immediately cut to thirty aircraft. These few did contribute to gunnery training, mainly in missions of Strategic Air Command at three locations. Other designs and tests of frangible ammunition occurred, some of much heavier projectiles. Such continuing developments are outside the scope of this work and are mentioned only in passing. Suffice it to say, the frangible bullet concept was legitimate. It is entirely conceivable that sometime in the future, it still could be employed in some fashion.

Flexible gunnery training was officially terminated (except by the Strategic Air Command) in September of 1945. By early 1946, most of the RP-63s had been placed in storage, ultimately to be sold for scrap, and for some time thereafter, Army arsenals bulged with useless frangible ammunition.

What did we learn from this short-lived training project? We learned many things, mainly that the concept was viable. It illustrated from what unlikely origins a critically important idea could come, and we found out the hard way how necessary it becomes in vital programs of this nature for diverse groups to cooperate. We saw here the unselfish dedication of universities, corporations and segments of the military, coming together to implement a device foreign to any of their experiences. These included Duke University, Princeton University, Michigan University, Bakelite Corporation, the Corning Glass Works, Sperry Gyroscope Company, Bell Aircraft Company, Wright Army Air Field, Aberdeen Proving Grounds, Air Training Command, Ordnance Department and, last but certainly not least, NDRC.

It demonstrated how red tape and tradition can pose stumbling blocks which, except for the total dedication and perseverance of two men, could have proven insurmountable to the success of a vital training device. And finally, it graphically demonstrated just how unprepared and badly organized we were for wartime research.

In 1948 the Office of Scientific Research and Development authored a World War II book titled *Rockets, Guns and Targets,* Brown and Little, publishers. At the end of chapter 30, "The Little Bullet That Didn't Hurt," we find this particular pertinent summation: ". . . valuable months were frittered away; perhaps a year was lost, or at least used less effectively than it might have been. In the last analysis, one or two willful men in the Ordnance Department nearly stopped the development altogether; one or two willful men outside the Ordnance Department kept it alive. This is too slender a thread on which to hang the fate of a research. It suggests a more independent procedure for the handling of possible future innovations of military value."

The pinball's granddaddy 8

The aircraft chosen to become the first "live" target for air-to-air gunnery training boasted a distinguished pedigree. When the first P-39 rolled off the Bell Aircraft assembly line in 1937, it created a sensation of sorts. Nothing like it had ever been seen and it promised performance that never quite materialized.

Its shortcomings were not the fault of the design, radical as it was for the time. Bell engineers had produced the ultimate in the tiny fighter—or so it was then believed. It had extremely clean lines with the fully enclosed, liquid-cooled Allison V-12 engine located *behind the pilot!* In addition, the little aircraft boasted innovative automobile-type doors on either side of the cockpit with roll-down windows.

The design marked a singular departure from all commonly accepted aircraft engineering concepts, but it had a definite purpose. By placing the engine, constituting a large part of the airplane's total weight, behind instead of ahead of the center of gravity, designers believed the smaller turning radius would improve the plane's aerobatic capability. Remember that the traditional dogfighting combat methods of World War I were still in vogue in the thirties. Only later did wartime experience demonstrate that maneuverability, while important enough, was not an absolute necessity in assessing an airplane's overall effectiveness. We have examples of the Lockheed P-38 and the Navy's fine Grumman fighters, none of which could begin to maneuver with the Japanese Zero but which, nonetheless, compiled an enviable record against that agile craft.

Ironically, the Airacobra, as first laid out on the designer's worksheets, represented a more traditional configuration. The Model 3 (never built) envisioned the pilot behind the engine and not too far ahead of the tail section. The engine was located over the center of gravity with a five-foot drive shaft running to a reduction gearbox situated immediately behind the propeller. This permitted the installation of four .50 caliber Brownings, or two .50s and one 25 mm cannon between the engine and propeller, the cannon extending through the prop hub.

Tricycle landing gear—very new at the time—was a prominent feature of this new design. The nose wheel was not fully retractable and would have required a bubble housing for streamlining purposes. The power plant, an Allison V-1710E-2, was equipped with a turbo-supercharger mounted beneath the engine, its waste gates exiting at the bottom of the fuselage. Four exhaust headers, two on each side, ran from the engine straight down to the turbocharger. The turbo intercooler shared a common fresh air duct with the oil

The XP-39 was the first Airacobra. Only one aircraft was built, after which succeeding modifications drastically curtailed its performance. It was the fastest of all the P-39 models, and its turbocharger permitted operation at high altitude. Most knowledgeable people today maintain that procurement "experts" ruined a potentially fine fighter. Smithsonian Institution

cooler, located between the engine and pilot's cockpit. The wing airfoil, an NACA 23018 at the root changing to 23009 at the tip, was quite thick and similar to the old Clark Y. It's obvious that an aircraft produced in this form would not have been very fast.

The XP-39 appeared remarkably soon after Bell drafted and abandoned the Model 3. Fortunately, many of the outmoded features of the latter were discarded and many of its innovations retained. These included a cleaned-up version of the tricycle gear, the supercharger and the drive shaft from engine to propeller. The drive shaft was extended sufficiently to permit repositioning of the cockpit behind the armament but ahead of the engine. This configuration characterized all of the subsequent Allison-powered Bell fighters.

With its sleek lines and turbocharged engine, the XP-39 was a fine fighter for its day and would have proven a formidable opponent for any aircraft then in operation. Unfortunately, Army brass took to meddling with the design (a continuing problem even in modern times), adding weight here and eliminating desirable features there, until the final product departed so far from the original that Bell engineers often became discouraged and exasperated. The P-39, in its later configurations, proved incapable of fulfilling more than a modest combat role for the United States when the drums of war sounded.

In the view of military pilots who flew the tiny fighter in combat, the biggest blunder committed by Army aviation brass was the elimination of the turbocharger, the mechanical marvel that made the P-38 and P-47 such successful high-altitude performers. The P-39 struggled to reach 25,000 feet, and at 30,000 it was all done. There have been instances of pilots exceeding this level, but not by much and with considerable difficulty. For all intents and purposes, it could not operate with any degree of efficiency over 15,000 feet.

Designers should not be faulted for the P-39's limited range—approximately two hours flight time under normal conditions; going to war emergency would drastically curtail that time. At this point in the aircraft evolutionary process no one foresaw the requirement for long-range escort fighters. High-level planners visualized single-seat combat airplanes of the day as interceptors, required only to take off, engage

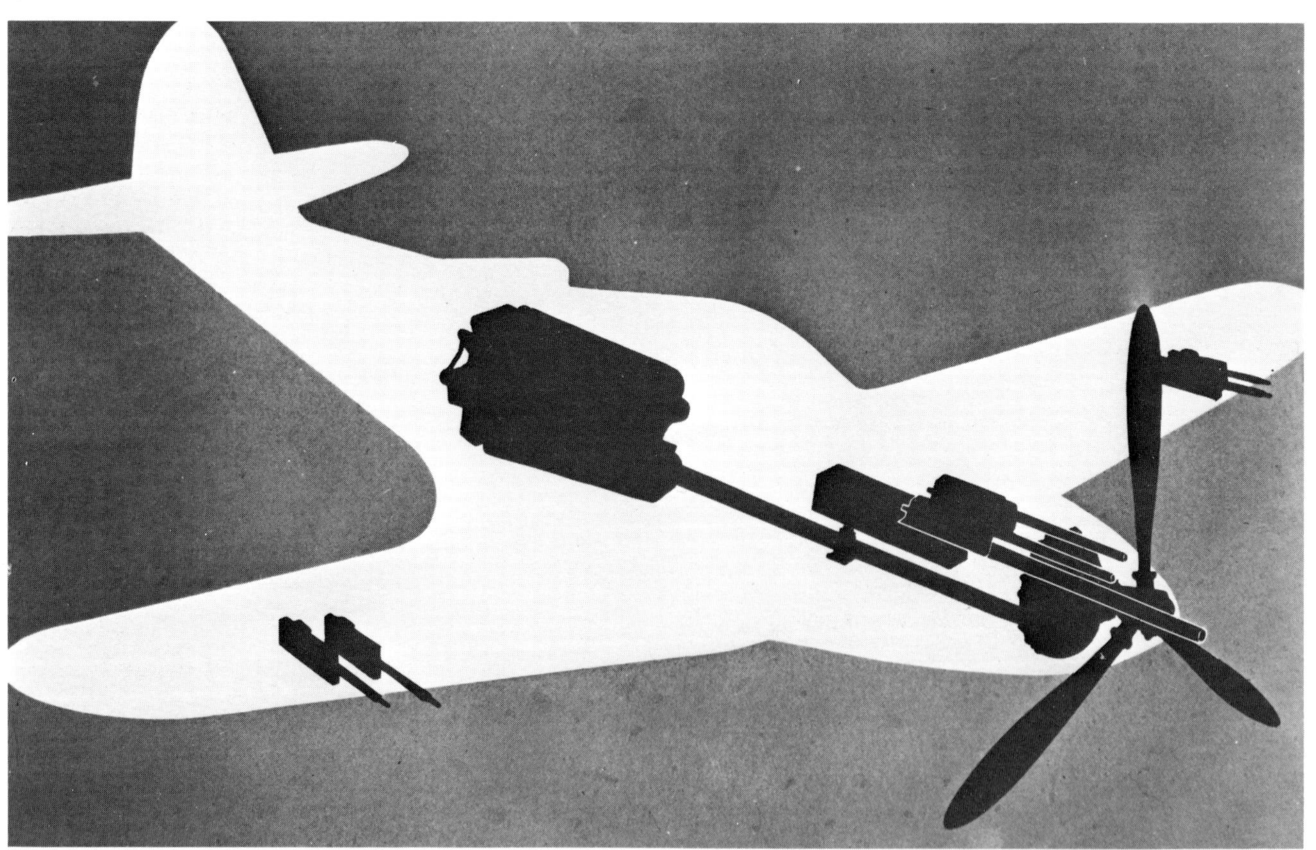

Arrangement of weapons and engine in most models of the P-39. Four .30 caliber Brownings are embedded in wings and two .50 calibers are located in fuselage nose, synchronized to fire through the propeller arc. A single 37 mm cannon barrel extends through the gearbox and hollow propeller hub. Later model (P-39Q) and all P-63s carried two .50 caliber machine guns in pods under the wings, replacing the .30 calibers. The cannon, heaviest weapon carried by any fighter during World War II, could be fired singly or in combination with the machine guns. This weapon's arrangement was made possible by placing the engine behind the pilot, driving the propeller by means of a ten-foot drive shaft connected to the gearbox in the nose. US Air Force

the enemy close in and return to a nearby base. The famous British Hurricanes and Spitfires, as well as the German Bf 109, were similarly limited. Only the Japanese were farsighted enough to design long-range capability into their Zeros, but here, with long overwater operations envisioned, mission dictated design.

The airfoil section selected for the P-39 also had some drawbacks. Though clean enough and ideally suited for speed at the time it was designed, it proved inefficient when asked to perform in high-g situations. It had a pronounced stalling tendency in steep turns or sharp pull-ups. Usually a pilot, entering a turn requiring more than moderate control stick back pressure, never knew whether he would make it around or high-speed stall at some point in the maneuver.

Despite the obvious drawbacks of the design, the P-39 proved very successful in the hands of Russian pilots. Colonel Alexandre Pokryshkin, the top Allied fighter pilot of World War II, obtained forty-eight of his fifty-nine victories in the P-39. His record proved the exception to the rule, although we also had some super pilots in the Air Force who ran up impressive scores with the Airacobra, strictly on individual skill. (It's interesting to contemplate what these men could have done with a P-51 or P-47.)

The P-39 carried either the 37 or 20 mm cannon, depending on model and user. The British, desperate for war equipment of all kinds early in the war, purchased 675 Bell aircraft, the P-39C modified per British demand and redesignated Model 14. When the aircraft failed to meet specifications, the English refused to use them in combat and turned 212 over to the Russians. They returned another 179 to the United States who sent them to Australia as the P-400. The primary difference between the modified airplane and the P-39C was in armament. The British insisted on a 20 mm cannon to replace the 37 mm all the rest of the P-39 models carried. In addition, the British added two .303 caliber Brownings in the wing to complement the cowl guns. The P-400s did well in the South Pacific, although they were eventually replaced when hotter fighters became available.

The Communists loved the 37 mm cannon and they used the P-39 to great advantage as a tank-buster against the invading Nazi hordes. They used the little fighter primarily in a ground support role in which high altitude performance was not a requisite.

More than 8,900 P-39s, extending through Model Q, were built during the six odd years the little fighter was in production (see Appendix B). Russia obtained the greater portion of the 7,000 N and Q models through Lend Lease; the rest went to Allied nations and our own Flying Training Command. The United States used them in limited fashion in North Africa where the German Bf 109s shot them down almost at will. In the South Pacific P-39 pilots were actually discouraged from seeking combat against the Japanese Zero, although they did perform creditably as we have seen. It all depended on the pilot, and we did have some good ones.

But it was in the Air Training Command that the P-39 proved its real worth. With the advent of the gun camera missions in the flexible gunnery training program, the tiny fighter was admirably suited to simulated low altitude curve of pursuit attacks. Pilots who flew the last model, the "Q", praised it as an excellent low altitude fighter. It is indeed ironic that the XP-39, the first Airacobra built by Bell, was rated highest in performance among all the models produced. It was

The P-39C. Only eighty were procured, although a modification, the English-ordered Model 14, was produced in relatively large number. A total of 675 Model 14s were delivered to the British. They differed from the P-39C mainly in armament. A 20 mm cannon was substituted for the 37 mm and the .50 calibers were replaced by the English .303 caliber machine guns. The P-39C carried all its armament in the nose. The English buried four .303s in the wings. The British were disenchanted with the Model 14 and gave all of them up after some tentative strafing missions were flown. The Russians were given 212 Model 14s and 179 were returned to the United States. These were redesignated P-400 and shipped to the South Pacific. Some of them served on Guadalcanal. Sixty of the original P-39Cs were converted to Ds and the "C" model never saw combat. Smithsonian Institution

My time in a P-39

The arrival of the first P-39 at Kingman Army Air Field injected a bit of excitement into an otherwise prosaic existence. My friend Guy Hawkins, who graduated with me in the class of 43-C at Luke AAF and who served with me at every base to which I was assigned during the war, ferried the first Airacobra to Kingman. According to my Form 5 (the official Air Force pilot log maintained by Base Operations), I was checked out by Hawkins in this plane, a P-39K, on April 10, 1944, and I departed that night for Barksdale AAF, Shreveport, Louisiana, to pick up another. Talk about the blind leading the blind!

I had perused and otherwise perfunctorily studied the P-39 Dash One and had experienced the thrill of my first flight in a high-performance airplane. I recall, with relish, my astonishment as that powerful Allison caught and fired, the little aircraft shaking on its gear before the engine smoothed out, the amazing (to me) acceleration on the takeoff run and the effortless lift-off. And the sight of that tremendous silver circle set up by the whirling blades of the largest propeller I had ever flown behind. I was truly in hog heaven!

The euphoria was short-lived. A tiresome train trip to Shreveport and then the dispiriting sight of an old, bedraggled "D" model I finally located in an isolated corner of the airfield. Please dear Lord, I prayed, don't let them put me in this thing! They did, of course, and I found out, not surprisingly, that this bird had come from a combat zone, the Pacific I think, and was completely bereft of navigational equipment. It took some earnest persuasion to coax a bored, uninterested communications buck sergeant to install a small, low-frequency receiver on the cockpit floor. It was a Motorola, I remember, with a knob and pointer that could be turned between 200 and 400 kilocycles, the band of the radio ranges of that day. I could barely reach the tuning and volume controls at its location under my right leg. A five-channel VHF, the first I had ever seen and which was just being installed at military bases stateside, provided my only means of communication.

The airplane was equipped with a centerline 64-gallon external fuel tank which gave me less than 3½ hours' flight time, maximum, not much considering the distance I had to travel and the terrain over which I would fly. I was in base operations planning my route and refueling stops when it suddenly occurred to me that I just wasn't ready for this ambitious undertaking. I had plenty of cross-country experience in the old standby AT-6, but this fighter was a different proposition. Right then I would have given a lot for a few more hours' indoctrination in the P-39. That 40-minute checkout flight was inadequate, to say the least.

I had to do it, of course, so off I went. Surprisingly, everything went smoothly at first and I was beginning to enjoy myself, although I confess to momentary consternation when the auxiliary tank ran dry. The silence occasioned by the disruption of that powerful Allison's roar was most disconcerting. I switched to a full wing tank and the sound of that big engine coming to life was comforting music to my ears. Then, a short time later, things came completely unglued.

I was coming up on Abilene, some 345 statute miles from Barksdale and a bit over one hour en route. During the last ten minutes I had been receiving some uneasy vibes; something was wrong but it took me too long to identify the trouble. The first indication was a gradual increase in propeller rpm, necessitating numerous adjustments of the pitch control. Inexperience in the airplane and downright stupidity prevented me from identifying the problem immediately and only after my rpm crept over 3,000 and pitch control had reached its farthest limit did I finally conclude I was in trouble. I had to find a landing field—and right soon! The P-39 refused to maintain altitude with a runaway prop, and this was becoming very serious.

Abilene Army Air Field (Dyess Air Force Base today) lay to the west of the city and from a distance I knew immediately I couldn't make it. I was now descending, and fairly rapidly, from my original altitude of 10,000 feet. My only chance was Abilene Municipal Airport, southeast of the city and much closer. I managed to quell a rising panic as I prepared for an emergency landing there. My "Mayday" went unanswered and this did little to ease my mind. I began reviewing emergency procedures (the few I could remember) as I began searching the still unfamiliar cockpit for controls I knew I'd need. I lifted the nose to decrease airspeed, flipped the landing gear switch to the down position and set up a downwind leg at 2,500 feet parallel to the north-south runway. Surprise! No gear! It took a while for that to sink in and when it did, I realized I no longer had an electrical system. I then recalled that the Dash One had made quite a point of the fact that everything on the aircraft was electrically operated. Gear, flaps, lights, radio, propeller pitch . . . everything!

Well, I thought, that's not so bad. I'll just lower the gear manually. I reached for the hand crank at the right of my seat, but I couldn't rotate the blamed thing; it wouldn't budge. In desperation I drew my right foot back and kicked the handle—hard! The mechanism came unstuck and I started winding. I don't remember how many revolutions it takes to extend the P-39 gear in this manner, but I can tell you it seemed like an eternity before the wheels "thunked" into the locked position. I had no warning lights, of course, so I didn't know if I had a "green" or not. No matter; I had to land.

I had almost completed my turn to final by this time, a bit hot and with plenty of altitude to clear the power lines on the north edge of the field. I reached for the flap switch. Another surprise! Of course, I had no flaps either and the runway was coming up fast. And to add to my troubles, an Army BT-13 was just wheeling onto the active ahead of me preparing for takeoff. Problems were multiplying fast; I had now committed myself and couldn't go around. There was only one thing to do . . . and I did it.

I remember slipping violently (we were cautioned not to do this with a P-39) as I crossed the power lines, keeping my nose up and desperately trying to bleed off excess airspeed. I managed to "spike" the little fighter down just ahead of the now-rolling trainer and violently applied my brakes. The end of the 5,000-foot runway was coming up fast and the right brake burned out right at the end. That put me in a mild ground loop to the left and my right wingtip just cleared the tail section of an airlines DC-3 sitting on the taxiway just clear of the active.

It had been a near thing and I was thankful indeed to be down in one piece. I contacted the Army Air Field right away and a maintenance truck arrived shortly. They found that the generator had burned out, a condition I would have ascertained had I been properly observant of ammeter indications. Loss of electrical power to the propeller pitch motor had allowed the prop blades to flatten out, increasing rpm to such an extent that there was no longer sufficient pulling force to keep the plane airborne.

Incidentally, the errant BT-13 went tooling off into the boonies when I usurped the takeoff runway. I met the instructor during my thirty-six-hour stay at Abilene and he told me it had been a terrifying experience. There were some eight or nine aircraft over from the WASP flying training field at Big Springs shooting landings at Abilene that day, and my emergency created quite a stir among the girls. I told the instructor, a likable second lieutenant, I was sorry but I had no way to communicate with civilian towers and most stateside aircraft, even if my electrical system had not been out. VHF equipment, we agreed, was still pretty new, and he sheepishly admitted he should have cleared the traffic pattern before taking the active. They say we learn from experience. I'd much prefer to obtain my learning in some other fashion.

My emergency occurred at 4 p.m. on April 13 and I finished my trip on the 15th without further incidence. I cleared out for Luke Field right after the maintenance people from Abilene Army Air Field replaced the generator and brakes of my aircraft. It was a short hop from Luke up to Kingman and I can truthfully say I was glad to be home.

I guess I profited as much from that ill-fated cross country as anything else in my military flying career. Ironically, I experienced the same type malfunction at a later date with a P-63 on a camera mission. This time I detected the problem right away and returned to home base with no trouble. One difference between the two airplanes involved the propeller. The Kingcobra's had a four-blade hydraulic prop compared to the electric three-blade on the P-39. Gear and flaps on the P-63 operated electrically like the Airacobra. I became a firm believer in proper checkout procedures, and I determined right then that I would never again feel ill at ease in the cockpit of a new airplane.

Whenever anyone asks me what my favorite military aircraft was, I unhesitatingly pick the P-39. My career bridged the two distinct eras of conventional and jet-powered airplanes and, while I enjoyed flying the jets, the tiny little fighter of World War II days brings back the fondest memories. In terms of pure flying pleasure, it truly was the most enjoyable. Flying only training missions with no high altitude requirements and without the necessity of performing violent combat maneuvers, the Airacobra was an exceptionally fine aircraft. And, despite claims to the contrary, it was an agile aerobatic airplane. I've done everything in that little bird you could imagine and I've never come close to having trouble. Loops, spins, rolls, both slow and snap (the latter strictly forbidden but we did them anyway)—you name them, I've done them all! As long as one remembered to keep the nose down on stall and spin recovery and to be moderately careful in low altitude turns, there was absolutely no problem.

Kingman obtained a two-seat training version of the Airacobra, designated TP-39, shortly after the single-seaters had been delivered, and this provided hours of entertainment and gave us the opportunity to carry passengers. It took a brave soul to go up in that machine, believe me. An additional seat was squeezed into the nose ahead of the main cockpit. It was very tight, and not everyone could fit in it. The passenger had to straddle the propeller driveshaft with his feet resting on either side of the reduction gearbox. Limited to a chest pack parachute (the back and seat types were too bulky), he couldn't attach the chest pack to the parachute harness while in flight. He had to lay the chute under the canopy behind him, interfering somewhat with the forward visibility of the pilot. All in all, a somewhat crude adaptation but one which provided enjoyment of a different kind. I've often wondered what the passenger would have done in an emergency; I doubt that he could have bailed out, but this ominous possibility didn't faze a whole host of ground-pounders who jumped at the chance to fly in the Airacobra.

We were cautioned that the center of gravity of the two-seater could be considerably outside the acceptable limits for flight, depending on the weight of the passenger. We were warned to fly it straight and level only and to never, but *never* attempt aerobatics in it. Of course, most of us ignored that warning and found that the TP-39 would perform most maneuvers just as well as the single-seaters. I've done spins in this odd aircraft with a tiny WAC in front (she was a link instructor and eligible for flight time) and experienced no unusual flight symptoms at all. This held true with all the passengers I carried; weight and size had no apparent effect on performance or flight characteristics.

In May of 1944 I was assigned TDY (temporary duty) to the Fixed Gunnery Instructors School at Matagorda Peninsula, Texas, for aerial and ground gunnery training. Upon completion of the one-month course I returned to Kingman and set up a gunnery school to provide proficiency training for the fighter pilots assigned to our station. This was supposed to keep us combat ready, or so they told us. Few of us ever got the opportunity to demonstrate our skills but we kept in shape nonetheless. We flew our gunnery missions out of Site Three, one of the auxiliary fields located just north of Route 66 about 30 miles northeast of Kingman AAF. I scheduled five pilots each week during the three months our training program existed, and we all practiced gunnery in the P-39.

The little fighter had some idiosyncrasies. When firing .50s with the "Q" model using the underwing pods, we could detect yaw whenever one gun jammed. This didn't happen too often but I experienced it down at Matagorda. It was strange, watching the sight drift off the target, especially when firing ground gunnery. The airplane was so small and the gun so powerful.

It made a good platform for hunting coyotes and we did a bit of that. Got a few, too. We also enjoyed chunking 37 mm shells along the desert floor. We weren't supposed to have any of that ammunition, but our armorers managed somehow. It was a pleasant interlude, and profitable. All of us eventually returned to flying camera missions but we missed the informal camaraderie we had at Site Three.

Three enlisted men lived at the site. They loaded ammunition and tended targets. We took turns towing the sleeves and banners, duty that could prove interesting, especially when a buddy would stay in his curve of pursuit down to an extremely small angle-off, firing all the while. I can't recall that any of our fighters ever picked up any bullet holes, but I know there were some close shaves.

We were getting a number of returned combat fighter pilots at Kingman toward the end of 1944. Some of them (a minority, fortunately) seemed to take pleasure in deprecating the abilities of those who had never been overseas. As if our bad luck in that regard weren't enough, they managed to rub salt in the wound, so to speak. We stoutly defended ourselves at the bar or poker table, knowing full well that we could fly just as well as these "hot rocks." On many occasions some of us accepted challenges, knight-errant style, to do combat with the experienced gladiators, using motion picture cameras as weapons. Results of some of these aerial duels proved embarrassing to some combat returnees after observing the pictorial evidence. Those who flew the old fighters will remember these cameras. They were activated by a trigger on the stick. Exposed film could be processed and projected on a screen, allowing a pilot's mission to be assessed and graded. Those of us who flew gun camera and pinball missions always carried film aloft to check on the accuracy of our passes. I still have quantities of this film which, due to the ravages of time, is today practically unreadable.

I well remember one occasion when braggadocio reached tragic limits. A particularly "hot" combat veteran became somewhat obnoxious at the bar one night. He taunted one of my more impulsive acquaintances which resulted in a challenge to do battle the next day. A wager was involved, the type and amount I can't recall, but it became downright ridiculous when the combat vet insisted on flying a P-39, giving my friend the advantage of a P-63. It was a silly gesture; in view of the consequences we all wish it had not been made.

The two went at it the next afternoon. Another friend and I were waging our own little war up north of Site Three when we heard the first radio communication indicating that something was wrong somewhere. It was the voice of our combative friend a few miles away imploring his opponent to "Get out! Leave it, for God's sake!" A few seconds later we heard him again, this time with a note of finality and despair, "Oh, my God! He didn't make it." He next called the Kingman tower, giving details of the mishap and the location.

My partner and I headed for the area and when we arrived we found our friend circling at about 2,000 feet above the rough terrain, the object of his attention plain to see. There on the desert floor, was a P-39. At first glance it appeared to be intact but, of course, it wasn't. It had fallen, turning like a falling leaf in the deadly flat spin; it obviously had struck with little forward motion. A couple hundred yards behind trailed the collapsed canopy of a parachute to which was attached the body of the unfortunate combat veteran. What most of us suspected might happen had become a reality. The combat pilot, attempting to turn with our friend in the superior P-63, stalled and foolishly attempted to recover with insufficient airspeed. We, who had been flying the little fighter for some time, were fully aware of the Airacobra's flat spin idiosyncrasies, but this pilot, coming from the cockpit of a P-51, a much more forgiving aircraft, had, in the heat of the contest, forgotten the warnings given in all checkout briefings and indoctrinations. He paid for the oversight with his life. A lesson dearly bought, it remained a graphic reminder to others inclined to forget. It was patently impossible for a P-39, given approximate parity in pilot skills, to engage in combat with a P-63 on anything approaching even terms.

capable of 390 mph top speed (Bell claimed 400) at a modest 6,204 pounds. Compare this with the Model Q which grossed at 8,300 pounds with a top speed five mph less than its ancestor. Allison powered all the P-39s, ranging from the V-1710-30 of 1090 horsepower to the 1350 hp V-1710-47 in the XP-39E, the test bed for the experimental P-63.

A moderately experienced low-horsepower pilot of today would find the P-39 an immensely enjoyable aircraft to fly, if mindful of a few simple precautions. The controls were extremely light, but the Airacobra was notoriously tricky in the hands of a careless operator. The slightest lateral pressure on the control stick would send the ball (part of the familiar turn and bank indicator) skidding unless coordinated properly with rudder. The P-39 retains the unenviable reputation of pilot killer. Although many who flew and loved the little airplane will hotly dispute that assessment, the sad fact remains that too many inexperienced pilots met their fate during operational training, mostly in the landing pattern. The final turn, at relatively low airspeed and with all the garbage out—gear and flaps extended—is most conducive to inattention on the part of a complacent operator. The upcoming runway can become a fixation; anticipation of overshooting the landing strip while in the final turn often induces a tendency to feed in too much bottom rudder. In the case of the Airacobra, this could result in a sudden snap roll, generally fatal at traffic altitude.

One other characteristic leading to some serious complications, was the P-39's tendency to flat spin. This was unrecoverable, as demonstrated many times during the war. It was usually caused by bringing the nose up too soon recovering from a normal stall or spin. The little fighter would perform all the requisite maneuvers safely and with no problem, as long as the pilot remembered to attain adequate airspeed before regaining straight and level flight. Other than this, the P-39 was a normal airplane in all respects. The experienced "throttle jockeys" learned early on to keep the ball centered on final turn and to keep the nose down recovering from a stall or spin.

Typical of pilots' reactions to the P-39 is that of John A. Aranyos, who writes: "After a combat tour in Europe as a Zemke Zipper in P-47s and fresh from R & R (rest and recuperation) in Miami, my first stateside assignment was to Yuma (By Gawd!), Arizona. I consider my stay at Yuma from 21 January to 9 May, 1945 one of the memorable highlights of my military career. Many of the combat-experienced pilots assigned to duty at Yuma opted not to fly the pinball and were subsequently assigned to other bases. As for me, I jumped at the chance to stay in fighters, in spite of the questionable mission that went with it.

Qualifying to fly the pinball was, to say the least, a very informal program. First, a cockpit check in the Airacobra with a few words on airspeed and stalls, a pat on the back and I was off into the blue Arizona sky. There were three more flights in the P-39 for familiarization, then seven flights of curve of pursuit 'attacks' on the bombers, each pass being recorded by my gun camera."

Ed Wakeland spent some interesting months flying B-26s in Africa and, in November of 1944, he was assigned to Harlingen. He was one of the few "multifan" pilots to fly fighters in the flexible gunnery training program. He remembers his P-39 check-out with pleasure: "I came back to the United States in November of 1944. At that time I flew tow-target missions in B-26 bombers [actually, AT-23s] until we received the P-39. [Harlingen, as well as the other flexible gunnery training bases, obtained P-39s as early as April of 1944.] I read the T. O. (Technical Order, in this case the Dash One), got the crew chief to crank it up and took off. All I can remember is it had warning signs about what not to do, starting from the right and going all the way to the left of the cockpit. It was a very small cockpit; however, it was a very nice airplane to fly. It would do rolls probably as good as the P-63. The nose never wobbled. . . ."

It should be noted that all pinball pilots were checked out in the P-39 prior to their flights in the P-63 and the RP. Because the Kingcobra was so superior, comments in regard to the P-39 are relatively scarce among pinball pilots. This is understandable, but talk to one who flew only the P-39 and you'll receive some outstanding reports. Used in the manner for which it was best suited, the P-39 was a remarkable aircraft.

P-39Qs stacked up in echelon. The last model produced prior to the P-63, the "Q" is readily identified by the machine guns mounted in pods under the wings. The P-39Q was the first Bell fighter to emply the interconnected throttle-prop pitch concept. With this system, propeller rpm changed with throttle adjustment. Some pilots liked it, some didn't, but most never got used to it. Smithsonian Institution

The P-39F was basically a P-39D with minor modifications. An Aeroproducts constant speed propeller was substituted for the Curtiss-Electric and this improved reliability. Only 229 Fs were procured, most of which supported the "Torch" landings in North Africa. The "F" became easy prey for the Bf 109. Smithsonian Institution

One of the many Airacobra modifications, the P-39E was test bed for the forthcoming P-63. Heaviest of the P-39 models, it grossed out at a whopping 8,918 lbs. It was powered by the Allison V-1710-47 rated at 1350 hp, the highest powered Bell fighter until the P-63D. The first Bell product to employ the laminar flow wing, only three were produced and none saw combat. Smithsonian Institution

The P-39D was the first Bell fighter procured in substantial numbers (863) and was the first Airacobra introduced into combat. Its record was not impressive. Note that the two .30 caliber machine guns originally located in the nose are now embedded in the wings. Note fuel tank shackles underneath the fuselage. Smithsonian Institution

Bell comes up with a winner 9

Slightly more than a year after the P-39 went into full production, Bell engineers and designers got together to consider producing a new fighter. With increasing evidence of the Airacobra's combat limitations and recent advances in aeronautical design to draw upon, they believed they could develop an exciting new airplane offering almost unlimited potential.

A brand new airfoil section, the so-called laminar flow which derived its superior characteristics primarily from the location of its maximum thickness (much farther rearward than on conventional wings), was chosen for the new design. This proved to be a most judicious decision. Wind tunnel tests had shown that the laminar flow section produced much less turbulence moving through the air, hence less drag. Its superiority was proven in combat by the P-51, arguably the finest single-engine aircraft on either side during World War II and the first fighter to employ the new wing. The Mustang's record against the best the Axis powers could muster provides one testimonial to the effectiveness of the laminar flow.

Work began on the new Bell design in April of 1941, but the initial effort produced something less than desirable. The aircraft, as originally envisioned, had a projected gross weight of some five tons, whereupon the engineering staff apparently lost interest and shelved the whole thing, only to resurrect it in a hurry after Pearl Harbor.

This time the Army presented Bell with a set of specifications, including a gross weight limitation of 7,500 pounds and a maximum wing loading of 30 pounds per square foot with the laminar flow. Bell designers went back to their tables. They designated the project XP-63 and work was begun, using the basic P-39 configuration as a starting point. They retained the tricycle gear and the engine remained behind the pilot. They also kept the automobile-type doors, and this configuration held true for all subsequent P-63 models except the "D". (This one-of-a-kind fighter sported a bubble canopy.) With these similarities, the comparison with the P-39 ended.

Among the significant changes were installation of a more powerful engine, redesigned control surfaces and improved cooling ducts. All P-63s employed four-bladed, hydraulically controlled propellers. Other changes (mostly structural) were made, but the final product, similar in appearance to its progenitor, was an entirely different and superior aircraft. There were minor changes in armament. The 37 mm cannon was retained, as were the two .50 caliber synchronized machine guns in the nose, but two additional .50s were mounted in pods under the wings (similar to the P-39Q) on all models after the XP.

An important change, as far as the pilots were concerned, involved the propeller pitch control. All of the 63s, including the later RPs, synchronized the throt-

The P-63A was the first operational model of the Kingcobra. It was also the first to be converted to a pinball. Over 1700 model As were built, the majority of which went to Russia. Of comparatively short range, the P-63 did not fit into our long-range fighter concept but, with the 37 mm cannon, was ideally suited for a ground support role. The Russians destroyed great numbers of German tanks with this fighter. Smithsonian Institution

The P-63D, only Bell fighter fitted with the popular bubble canopy. Only one model "D" was built. Note machine gun pods under wings and adjacent external tank hangers. This was typical P-63 configuration. US Air Force

tle with propeller pitch, a modification begun with the later versions of the P-39Q. With the two connected, propeller pitch changed in direct ratio to throttle setting, and the familiar pitch control was missing from the quadrant. Only throttle and mixture remained, and some pilots, used to the common system, never felt comfortable with the new control.

In the P-63C, next to the "A" model the most numerous of the Kingcobras, synchronization produced rpms of 1,600 to 1,700 at twenty inches of manifold pressure, increasing to the maximum of 2,900 to 3,000 at fifty-five inches. With the Allison V-1710-117, the P-63's normal takeoff power was 55 in., dry, limited to five minutes or less. With the throttle advanced beyond 58 in., the water injection switch automatically cut in and boosted power to wet war emergency of seventy-six inches. In the Training Command water injection was not needed, of course, so throttles were safety-wired at fifty-five inches.

The P-63 was undeniably a fine fighter, attested to by those who flew and compared it with the P-51, P-47 or the P-38. Up to 15,000 feet it would outperform the P-51 in at least two categories, climb and maneuverability. In regard to the latter, the Kingcobra was particularly outstanding. P-63s have actually turned inside AT-6s, slower and supposedly tighter turning airplanes. It's interesting to contemplate how it would have fared against the famed Japanese Zero. Unfortunately, this comparison was never made.

Like its predecessor, the P-63's performance also suffered at altitude, although not to such an extent. Its Allison engines were different models from the ones carried by the P-39 and superior in performance. The proposed XP-63B (it was never built) was designed to carry the Packard V-1650 of 1,400 horsepower. This American version of the famed Rolls-Royce, the engine which powered the fine British fighters, the speedy Mosquito, and the Lancaster bomber, was manufactured under license by the Packard Motor Company here in the United States. One may contemplate, at some length, what kind of performance the P-63 would have displayed with this powerplant. Nonavailability was the official reason the Kingcobra was denied the Packard, but some cynics put the blame on General Motors, manufacturer of the Allison. This gigantic American corporation with its powerful lobbyists prevailed on military procurement personnel, some say, to restrict its Packard competitor to supplying engines only for the P-51. Pure speculation, but interesting nonetheless. At any rate, no performance specifications are available for the XP-63B and that's too bad.

The Allisons used in the P-63 employed an ingenious, entirely automatic auxiliary stage supercharger, which should have performed better than it did. A hydraulic fluid coupling supplied a smooth, flexible range of supercharger speeds dependent on the pressure altitude of the aircraft, quite a departure from standard design techniques of the day. It owed much to the recently developed automatic automobile transmissions, and while it performed the tasks for which it was developed in commendable fashion, it proved inferior to the supercharger used by the British Rolls-Royce and American Packard. No one can dispute the fact that the P-51 and the turbocharged P-47 and P-38 were superior performers at altitude.

One other shortcoming should be mentioned: limited range. The P-63's maximum internal fuel capacity of 132 US gallons (most models) restricted the aircraft to approximately two hours flight time at normal settings. This effectively reduced its role to intercept, ground support or training, but interception was no longer important. The new requisite, to an ever-increasing degree, was a long-range fighter capable of escorting our burgeoning fleets of bombers penetrating deep into the heartlands of Germany and Japan. Consistently flying eight-hour missions with wing fuel tanks that could be jettisoned, the P-51 filled the bill admirably. The P-63 was designed with a wet wing but Air Force specifications limited its internal fuel capacity, a result, it has been claimed, of powerful lobbying by North American and Republic Aviation. The P-63 could carry external tanks giving it good ferrying capability (flying time could be extended to six hours at normal cruise), but this was still insufficient in an escort role.

The P-63 excelled in the capacity of trainer, however. At the time the early models were going to Russia (1,952 Kingcobras went to our Communist ally), some were beginning to show up in flexible gunnery training bases throughout the United States. Pilots flying the P-39 transitioned into the newer aircraft and immediately began flying them on gun camera missions. The P-63 was outstanding in this capacity and became the stepping stone for the forthcoming RPs.

So they took some P-63As, deleted the armament and cockpit armor, replaced all of this with duralumin plates over the forward areas of the aircraft, and installed sophisticated—for that time—electronic counting gear in the nose. Thus was born the RP-63, the

On to the Kingcobra

I enjoyed the P-39 so much that checking out in the P-63 seemed no big deal at first. With this somewhat disinterested attitude, I approached my first flight in the Kingcobra. I found, to my surprise, that there was something definitely exciting about this fighter. Performance was breathtaking, especially in the climb, and the P-63 injected a new dimension into our practice dogfights. We could do things with the '63 that surprised many visiting firemen, especially the Marine jockeys who used to come over regularly from El Toro in their powerful F-4Us to test the merits of this strange new fighter.

We went right into gun camera missions with the P-63 at Kingman. Almost immediately we began hearing some disturbing reports about engine malfunctions in the "A" models, the only ones we had in late 1944. Some pilots at other bases, experiencing engine failure at altitude, had bailed out, resulting in the complete destruction of the aircraft, leaving accident investigators precious little with which to determine the cause of the problem. Maintenance people were in a quandry and with good reason. I learned later that Air Training Command almost grounded the entire fleet before I had my trouble.

It happened on a camera mission in October of 1944. From the onset of the flight I had trouble contacting any of the B-17s comprising our three-ship formation. This was not unusual. We liked to accuse them of tuning in local stations on their radio compasses as a means of alleviating the boring straight and level flying to which they were subjected. We fighter pilots were busy constantly, flying proper curves of pursuit (we were monitored and graded on our performance) for the benefit of the student gunners. We didn't like it one bit when the bomber jockeys tuned us out.

On this occasion I attempted to contact the lead bomber a number of times, trying to get them to close up a very loose formation. I had no luck and, in aggravation, finally pulled up close on the wingtip of the nearest B-17, throttling back to twenty inches in order to slow down. I eventually caught the attention of the copilot, patting my ear in the universal signal to establish radio contact. As I pulled away and added throttle, the Allison wouldn't take it, overloading and sputtering. It would smooth out only if I reduced throttle and each time I added power the condition worsened. I went through my emergency procedures, switching fuel tanks, changing mixture, anything that might give life to the balky power plant. At first it ran relatively well at twenty-two inches then, gradually less, and finally, almost at idle in order to run at all.

By this time I had pulled well away from my formation and when it became apparent I was not going to succeed in making that power plant behave, I prepared to bail out. I was all ready to jettison the right door when I noticed that I was still over the edge of a mountain range and obviously too low at that point to make it with any margin of safety. Just ahead, however, was a wide valley and I headed for it. By this time, the propeller was windmilling and I just managed to clear the last low ridge before an expanse of level desert appeared beneath me. I knew I was still too low to use my parachute and I prepared, with some trepidation I'll admit, for a gear-up forced landing.

So I set the aircraft down on the mesquite-dotted landscape and it was rough. I recall the bushes whizzing by just before touchdown and, after an eternity, a series of jolts as the plane touched and I was thrown violently forward into my shoulder harness. The fighter slued around about a quarter turn to the right and finally came to a stop with dust and debris filling the cockpit. I don't remember jettisoning the doors or unplugging my oxygen hose and radio leads, but I do recall running along the right wing and springing off, clear of the smoking aircraft. Nor do I remember lifting the Form One from its receptacle, but there I stood, aircraft log firmly in hand and feeling slightly foolish.

It took almost two hours but I was eventually picked up. It seemed much longer, waiting there in the late afternoon heat (yes, it was still pretty warm in October) before an AT-6 finally came skimming low over the desert terrain and found me. This was long after flight after flight of bombers and other assorted aircraft passed over without seeing me. I'll never understand what my three B-17s were doing in the meantime. I can only surmise they continued blithely on their way, tuned in to Kate Smith or jive from the local station.

There was an investigation of course, the kind the military always conducts following aircraft accidents and incidents. This, fortunately, gave the Air Force its first opportunity to examine an intact P-63 after it had experienced the mysterious malfunction. I later learned that an improperly designed float chamber in the huge Stromberg carburetor was found to be the cause of this and previous accidents. Fixes were devised and all Kingcobras were grounded for a time throughout Flying Training Command. After a relatively short period they were back in commission having received retrofits that solved the problem once and for all.

The arrival of the RPs created little interest at the main base, as I recall. Some of us had been tabbed for reassignment and were not sent to Yucca with the other fighter pilots. I received my first pinball flight at Kingman in February of 1945, just a checkout and indoctrination. The frangible bullet missions were still a couple months in the future. Except for a noticeable decrease in performance, I found the RP to be not too different from the P-63. For whatever reason, takeoff run was longer, turning radius wider and anyone contemplating even the more prosaic maneuvers had better be prepared to insulate himself with plenty of altitude.

Before I transferred from Kingman I had made only four flights in the RP-63. On the very day I received my change of station orders, I had another accident. We're all familiar with the term "accident prone." Some of the Kingman officials were beginning to believe I was, and I wasn't so sure myself. This last (and it was my last in more than twenty more years in the service) occurred in a pinball and it happened on the takeoff roll on April 1. My friends continually referred to my "April Fool" joke, but for a while that day, I could find nothing at all to laugh at.

Thumbing through some of the official records in my possession, I find in the station history of Kingman Army Air Field an interesting table. One item applies to my last mishap. In a report of aircraft accidents for the period March 1 to April 30, 1945, there is reference to a takeoff accident in an RP-63A. The cause is listed as "material failure" and under the column labeled "Remedial Action of Aircraft Accident Committee," is this notation: "A positive check of the nose wheel shimmy dampers on RP-63 type aircraft is made daily." The military have always insisted that similar accidents never recur, wishful thinking in most instances.

A shimmy damper, for those unacquainted with the term, is a small hydraulic device consisting of a piston in a cylinder operating much the same as an automobile shock absorber. It is installed on the nose gear strut of tricycle gear aircraft to prevent the nose wheel from wobbling, or shimmying. The effect of a malfunctioning damper on an aircraft's takeoff or landing roll is severe vibration. It's usually catastrophic to tricycle gear aircraft—as I can attest.

I had about seventy mph on my takeoff run that day when the damper let go. I was still on the ground, of course, and this tremendous vibration set in. The instrument panel shook so violently on its shock mountings that shattered glass from various instruments filled the cockpit. The rudder pedals vibrated so badly I couldn't keep my feet on them and, of course, I couldn't use my brakes. The whole aircraft shuddered and the noise was deafening.

At first I thought I had blown an engine or lost a prop blade and I automatically shut down power. Had I been able immediately to diagnose the trouble, I would have retracted the gear, but fear was uppermost in my mind and I was in no condition right then to rationalize anything.

At any rate the pinball continued on its erratic way, gradually veered to the right and finally left the runway. A drainage ditch ran parallel to the runway and I finally made my wobbling, bouncing way into it. The nose gear strut snapped, followed almost immediately by the right gear which sheared. The aircraft then proceeded to cartwheel, wing-over-wing, and after a couple gyrations came to rest, upside down, with a somewhat discomfited pilot hanging from his shoulder harness. I was uninjured, fortunately, but my ego suffered a beating. My next pinball flight came exactly two months later at Indian Springs AAF.

I remember an incident at that Las Vegas sub-base which further demonstrates the unforgiving characteristics of the RP. One of the returned combat pilots was checking out in the pinball and I guess he wanted to show all of us stateside jockeys what a real pilot could do. On his very first takeoff he brought the airplane off the ground after an abnormally short run and tucked his gear up immediately upon breaking ground. An observant tower officer, witnessing the event, realized that something was amiss and ordered the flyer to return to base. Our errant boy was well off in the distance, climbing normally and apparently all right, but he heeded the tower and returned. When he shut his engine down and the propeller stopped windmilling, we found the last six inches of each prop blade bent back at a ninety degree angle. A casual inspection of the runway revealed large nicks in the asphalt where the blades had touched. The pilot was forcefully reminded, once again, that the pinball did not behave like its more docile counterpart.

I picked up 38½ hours in the RP, mostly on pinball missions. I finished my wartime tour with a total of 230:30 in the three Bell fighters, including 95:10 in the P-39 and 96:50 in the P-63. I became intimately familiar with them and I loved them all.

fabled pinball that pilots either came to love or hate. A total of 332 pinballs were produced by the end of hostilities. There were 100 "A" and 200 "C" models with the RP-63 accounting for the remaining thirty-two. It's interesting to note that only the "G" model exceeded the gross weight of its P-63 counterpart (see Appendix B). The P-63A came off the production line weighing an even 10,000 pounds gross, while the RP-63A tipped the scales at 8,300. Similarly, the P-63C at 10,700 pounds exceeded the weight of its RP offspring by some 2,000 pounds. (Some dispute these figures and authoritative writers cannot agree. The reader is referred to Fahey, J. D., "U. S. Army Aircraft," First Edition, which supports the specifications contained herein. Military historians generally consider Fahey an excellent source.) Most of the pilots who flew pinballs are of the opinion that the weight of the additional armor accounted for its reduced performance. The answer may lie elsewhere.

The commonly accepted performance figures for the P-63 and RP-63 are almost identical in terms of top speed. This thought persists: the deletion of guns, ammunition and cockpit armor more than compensated for the addition of the comparatively lightweight duralumin plates added to the aircraft structure of the pinballs. The decrease in performance, other than speed, could then be accounted for only by changes in shape and configuration brought about by the attached armor plates. These undoubtedly caused airflow disruption over the hypercritical laminar flow airfoil, which could very well account for the sluggish feel and the decrease in climb and maneuverability together with an attendant increase in stalling speed.

The P-63 had stiffer controls than the P-39, but this detracted little from its performance. No pilot need fear a high-speed stall in the Kingcobra except in the tightest, low-speed turn. Full throttle produced an exhilarating rate of climb. Landing speed was mild, a trifle hotter than the P-38 with its ultra-efficient Fowler flaps, but much less than the sizzling 120 mph "over the fence" needed with the AT-23. Pilots flying the Bell fighters on training missions generally agree on the comparative merits of the P-39 and the P-63. With the pinballs, however, we find conflicting reactions ranging from "It wasn't so bad" to "It's a real dog!" Many adverse comments stemmed from an inherent dislike, bordering in some instances on downright fear, of the frangible bullet missions themselves. John Aranyos ran the gamut from initial apprehension to relief and downright enjoyment in the cockpit of the pinballs. Some returning combat flyers, however, absolutely refused to participate in the program, as John has previously reported.

Privileged to fly the first two pinballs at Laredo in the early part of 1945, Karl W. Edmondson reports: "We got our first straight P-63s in July of 1944 and a few of us checked out. Then we got two pinballs. They were painted orange and were named *Frangible Sal* and *Pinball*. The names were painted on the side (of the fuselage) when they arrived. I can't tell when I first flew the pinballs because my Form Five listed them as plain P-63s. My first flight in the P-63 was in August of 1944. Our Form Fives were maintained mostly by our friends from across the border and were really screwed up. In fact, I noticed the other day in reviewing mine, I was credited with 4:05 'X' (passenger) time in a P-40K. I don't know who was flying it because I was the only one in it.

"We also had an A-20 in the research program for a while. It only flew a few missions because the plexiglass nose kept getting busted up. Maybe they ran out of plexiglass nose cones. It was painted green and I am not sure about the armor. I did not fly the A-20."

Carl Weaver's introduction to the RP-63 differed a bit from most. A returned combat fighter pilot, Weaver had been assigned to Kingman AAF during the winter of 1944-45. Shortly after his arrival, he volunteered for temporary duty with the Ferry Command to deliver fighter aircraft to various locations throughout the continental United States. On his first assignment, he was directed to the Bell Aircraft factory. Reporting to the commanding officer of the Army detachment at the Niagra Falls, New York, airport, he was handed a Pilot's Manual (the aforementioned Dash One) and told to check out in the RP-63.

"I taxied onto the service runway in this RP . . . and began my first flight in this type fighter," Weaver says. "Everything was normal after takeoff until I noticed I had no airspeed indication. I flipped on the pitot heat and shortly thereafter had a normal airspeed reading. I cruised the local area, shot several touch and goes and returned to the line. Good bird! It seems that while taxiing out the very narrow taxiway with snow piled high on each side, I had packed both pitot static tubes with snow. The pinball had two (pitot) tubes because they were vulnerable to the frangible bullets. Each was hung low under the wings of the airplane on opposite sides and were not visible from the cockpit."

Over 1,200 P-63Cs were built, most of which went to Russia. The "C" model is readily identified by the ventral fin. Ernest R. McDowell

Barrie Davis was familiar with all of the Bell fighters. "It was when I was stationed at Las Vegas in 1945 that I flew the pinballs," he remembers. "We had P-39s, P-63s and RP-63s up at Indian Springs where the fighters were located. Most of us were combat veterans who had flown tours overseas. The duty was interesting and Las Vegas was a nice town to visit every night.

"I had flown the P-39s in Africa and had seen the Russians do things I had thought impossible with that

The RP-63G, shown here at Clovis Army Air Force Base, New Mexico, during the postwar period when the Strategic Air Command used the last pinball model in final frangible bullet training missions. Ernest R. McDowell

plane while we were on a shuttle mission to Russia, so I was happy to get back into it. The P-63 proved a real improvement with more cockpit room, more power and more maneuverability. I never tried it at altitude, but I doubt it could perform as well as the P-51, P-38 or P-47. When the Japs were sending balloons armed with firebombs across the Pacific and over this country, one of the P-63s eventually made it to a reported 40,000 feet trying to shoot a balloon down but couldn't reach it. In Italy I managed an indicated 50,100 feet in a P-51.

"The RP-63 flew well, provided you were smooth on the controls. It was really clad in armor which weighted it down pretty well. I do not know what its weight was. At the time, I enjoyed flying more than I did the statistics on the aircraft. If the plane got off the ground, I was satisfied.

"Some of us tried aerobatics in the RP-63. It handled well, as I said, but its weight could cause problems. It rolled nicely and would do nearly everything the P-63 could manage, except it required more airspace. One day I tried a loop, diving to a now-forgotten airspeed and pulling up and over the top. No problem. Coming down the back side of the loop, however, I found myself in a continuous high-speed stall. If I pulled back too tightly, the plane shuddered and headed faster for the ground. If I relaxed the pressure, it flew again but the airspeed carried me downward at a rate which threatened to dash me against the ground before I reached the bottom of the loop. Fortunately, a valley was beneath me and this gave me the extra altitude I needed to nurse that baby back to level flight. [Other pilots report similar experiences.]"

Ed Wakeland checked out in the P-63 at Harlingen shortly after qualifying in the P-39. His recollection of the P-63: "It was a dream to fly!" He maintains that with one-quarter flaps it would outturn any aircraft in the air at that time.

Wakeland was introduced to the pinball in spectacular fashion. "We read the Dash One, climbed in and took off. It was quite an experience. I only did one thing in that bird that still gives me sweaty palms. I did a 'Split S' from about 17,000 feet and fell 8,000 before I could get it leveled out. Naturally I quit looking at the airspeed indicator when it passed the red line. I was nothing but an orange streak, throttle off and flying all over South Texas trying to slow down. Oh yes, that was the last time I tried that little trick!"

Tony Greget was another pilot well-acquainted with Bell products. Greget graduated from Luke Army Airfield in June of 1944 and transferred to Kingman the following August. "When I got to Kingman," he writes, "I checked out in the P-39 and started flying pursuit curves against B-17s in the gun camera program. Later I graduated to the P-63 Kingcobra (a beautiful, honest aircraft) and this continued until January of 1945."

Greget was transferred to Yucca Air Field, Kingman's main sub-base, when it was decided to transfer fighter operations there. He remembers, "Aside from flying our scheduled missions, we could pretty much fly anytime we wanted, day or night, for proficiency, of course. The poor Grand Canyon and most of the towns along the Colorado River did catch hell!"

Greget witnessed the arrival of the first RP-63 at Yucca and he's convinced from the first demonstration that there wasn't much wrong with this armored fighter. "Captain John Kropenik was selected to pick up the first aircraft. We had heard the bird was restricted to sixty degrees of pitch or bank because of additional weight, change of CG, etc. Knowing John, we were anxious to see him bring in the first one. We were not disappointed when he came in on the 'red line' on the deck and pulled up into an Immelman, followed by other gyrations. There went the restrictions!"

John N. Behrens was another pinball pilot stationed at Las Vegas (Indian Springs) during the frangible bullet training program. "Of course you are well aware that many years have passed since we took off at 200, cruised at 200 and landed at 200," Behrens writes, employing a bit of tongue-in-cheek hyperbole. "To give us confidence, the Bell Aircraft people sent one of their hot rock test pilots to Indian Springs to show us how easy it was to roll that thing right down on the deck. As I recall, one of our fighter pilots tried it about a week later. He made it, but barely. He scared himself so badly he turned in his wings to his older brother who was some sort of operations type there at the Springs."

Memories abound of more lighthearted moments, like the time Merlyn Franck and some of his compatriots awaited the arrival of the first P-63s at Laredo. According to Franck, "We were feeling like real 'smoldering boulders' because we were getting the hottest fighter in the AAF. When the first one arrived we were all anxiously waiting on the ramp. As the ship came to a stop and the pilot got out, removed *her* helmet and shook out *her* long blond hair, you never saw such a bunch of deflated egos. The pilot was, of course, a WASP (Women Airforce Service Pilot), one of the many females trained by the Army during the war to fly support type missions and ferry aircraft.

"Most pilots who flew the P-39 didn't have any problems with the RP-63," Franck maintains. "The whole secret was to keep your airspeed up and a little power on until touchdown. A fellow pilot there at Laredo once neglected this bit of advice and allowed his airplane to get too slow on final. He dropped the RP in so hard it drove both main gear struts up through the wing."

The Air Force made an ideal choice in its selection of the P-63 as the designated target aircraft. Some claim that the P-63 was a compromise and not really suited for its tasks. They are clearly in the minority. First, it was an excellent performer in a program requiring no high altitude capability; second, it was available for training missions without degrading our combat strength; and third, it was easier to configure to its armored posture than any of our engine forward airplanes. It thus became the target for frangible bullet training with a minimum of rebuilding. It remains an object of nostalgic memory to many old pilots who proudly claim the honor of once flying the pinball.

What was it really like? 10

Colonel John W. Persons was commanding officer at Tyndall Army Air Field when the first pinball missions were flown at that field. Headlines in the March 24, 1945, issue of the base newspaper the *Tyndall Target* bannered the following: "C. O. to Fly P-63 on First Frangible Mission Here." On April 1, Col. Persons did just that, and a subsequent issue of the same publication contained the story of the historic first, quoted here in part:

"An opportunity that comes to few enlisted men fell to S/Sgt. Merrill A. Tolbert, of Montgomery, Alabama, when the first demonstration of the newly-adopted frangible bullet was put on at Tyndall last Friday. Tolbert was firing .30 caliber machine guns, and his target was his commanding officer, Col. John W. Persons, completing his 6,000th hour of flying time by flying the first frangible bullet mission.

"Tolbert, a veteran of the European Theater of Operations, flew 32 night missions with the RAF and 28 daylight missions with the Eighth Air Force. In commenting on the frangible bullet, he said, 'That was the first time I ever shot at my CO. This new bullet will certainly help our gunners prepare for combat because it gives them the *feel* of aerial fighting, something I never got until we actually met the enemy. I think if we had had this bullet in the early days of gunnery, the aerial war would have been won by now. . . .'

"Col. Persons flew the first 'attack' against the B-24, and received numerous hits which spattered harmlessly against the armored plate and bullet proof glass of his RP-63. He was followed a few minutes later by Capt. Victor W. Schultz, of Benton Harbor, Mich., veteran P-51 pilot with 60 combat missions to his credit, who flew in behind Col. Persons in surprise follow-up attacks. The bomber's guns also scored 'kills' on Capt. Schultz' plane.

"Col. William H. Hanson, of Gallup, New Mexico, director of training and operations, fired the first shots with the frangible bullets.

"High praise for the new training device came from Col. Persons. 'The target airplane performed very smoothly,' he said. 'The guns in the bomber functioned well, and, in my estimation, our first mission was very successful. It is obvious that the type of training to be derived from the frangible bullet will be of vast benefit in the preparation of our gunners for combat.'"

Despite Col. Person's vast experience, it's questionable whether he should have been flying target missions at all. John Gornell brought this interesting assumption to light in a recent letter: "Scuttlebutt had it that due to Col. Person's known bad eyesight, there was some reluctance among B-24 crews and gunners to fly and shoot at the colonel's RP-63 for fear that he might fly right on through the B-24 on one of his fighter passes." An understandable reluctance, considering that many of the younger pilots possessing much better physical attributes did bore in to exceptionally close range on many of their passes.

Col. Person's rosy evaluation of his frangible bullet mission is at variance with many other early reports where results were not so satisfactory, but most agreed there was more good than bad in the program. In April of 1945, the future prospects of pinball training were indeed excellent.

Tony Greget remembers flying pinball missions at Kingman and his memory does not exactly coincide with Col. Person's report. As Greget tells it, "They wouldn't let us make any head-on passes for obvious reasons, so all we did were high-side and level-side (pursuit curve) passes. I do remember that if you made a normal pursuit curve you very seldom got any hits. So, being young, we wanted to get hits and did this by hanging in the pursuit curve with a low rate of closure and pressing in beyond minimum range. You can guess

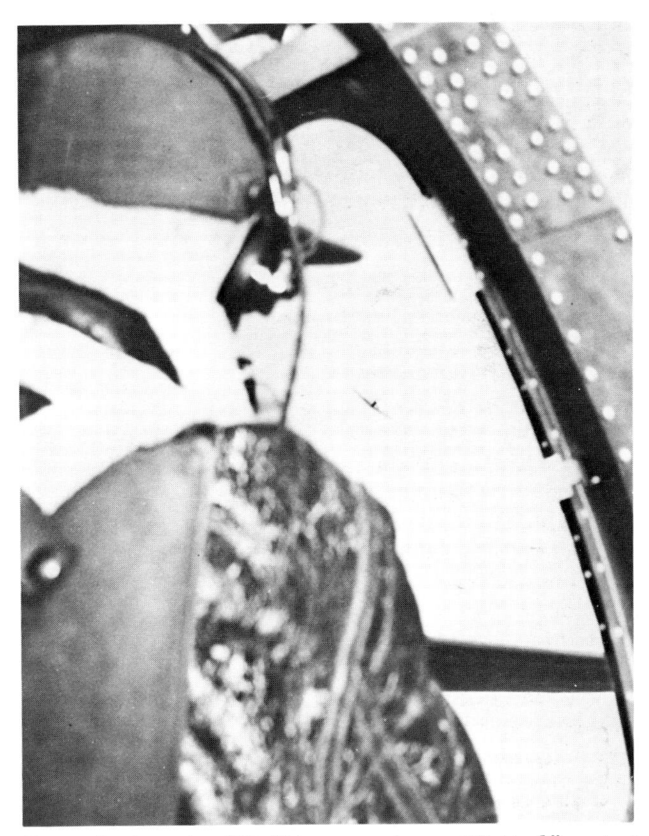

Gunner's view of an RP-63 in curve of pursuit "attack" against a B-17. It's interesting to note that this pass is being made on the left side of the bomber. Most were from the right. US Air Force

Three RP-63As stepped up in echelon. These pinballs display two types of carburetor air intakes. The middle aircraft has a flush intake, the other two sport the clamshell type. Ernest R. McDowell

what happened then. Hits on oil coolers, front windshields, cracked windows, hitting door hinges and springing the doors open, and various hits and damage to the aircraft which resulted in a number of emergency landings. However, to my knowledge, we never lost an airplane shot down."

Kurt Kurtzman, following a tour of duty in Europe, managed to get himself shot down flying a pinball out of Tyndall. He believes the gunners were French. (There were a number of foreign students in training over here in 1945.) And Robert C. Corson, a crew chief on pinballs at Yuma, recalls the RP-63 pilots and their attitudes: "Typical anticipation of their first flight was traumatic: 'I'm gonna get shot down again!' But upon landing, they always wore smiles! The pilots seemed to find a feeling of invulnerability in those heavily armored doors and windows, particularly while watching the counter on the instrument panel clicking off hits. During preflight, I tested the solenoid pickups under the armored panels on the leading edges and nose, by banging on them with a hammer.

"I also remember several aircraft which didn't come back. They took a round through the louvers in the intake ducts to the oil coolers. There were no casualties I heard about. The planes just lost oil pressure [or coolant] and bellied in to the desert. There was lots of that around Yuma in those days."

Corson says the primary problem with the pinballs on the ground was overheating in the summer. This was typical of other liquid-cooled aircraft, especially the P-39 which was much worse than the P-63. Unlike automobiles, the airplanes in the pinball program had no fans to draw cooling air through the radiators, relying rather on airspeed to maintain an adequate flow through the cooling ducts. There were times when aircraft had to be towed to the end of the active runway and engines started there just prior to takeoff. Corson claims it was necessary to change spark plugs frequently on the Allison engines. They tended to foul quickly, causing rough idling and decreased power in flight.

John Aranyos' first pinball mission was memorable. "My first flight in the Kingcobra hardly prepared me for my following flight, a live frangible bullet mission in the pinball," he writes. "Taxi out was no different from the P-63, except for the crash and rescue trucks accompanying me to the takeoff runway. (All takeoffs and landings of the pinball at Yuma were made with the crash and rescue equipment standing by along the active runway.) Acceleration during the takeoff run was sluggish and most of the runway was behind me before I finally broke ground. However, after getting the gear up and obtaining some airspeed, it started acting more and more like the Kingcobra. The climb to 11,000 feet was somewhat laborious.

"I made rendezvous with my assigned bomber over the desert range. Positive identification was made with the bomber firing the proper flares. The gunner would be firing at me from the waist position of the bomber flying his course at 9,000 feet. I would start my pass at 11,000 feet and slightly ahead of the bomber. Lateral distance out was strictly a matter of judgment and would determine the rate of dive and roll into the bomber. Ideally, I would be between fifty-five and forty-five degrees angle off as I came into firing range. One thought came to mind: I had come through a tour of combat relatively unscathed, and here I was deliberately setting myself up as a perfect target for some eagle-eyed kid aspiring to be a topnotch gunner at my expense. I felt I was the world's greatest idiot!

"Coming into range of the gunner," Aranyas continues, "I was anticipating the sound of bullets impacting on the airplane. There was none! Either they were missing me or this was a dry run for them. My second pass was more precise, more coordinated, and still no shudder or sound of impact. During my breakaway I glanced down at my hit indicator. Lo and behold! It had registered fourteen hits and I hadn't even felt a single impact. From that point on the frangible bullet mission lost some of its fearsome awe; that is, until an incident on a later flight restored my respect for the graphite artillery.

"On that occasion, I had started my pass a little closer than usual and wound up within firing range with my nose pointed directly at the waist gunner. Suddenly, all hell broke loose in the cockpit! Bits and pieces of graphite went zinging and ricocheting beneath my seat and rudder pedals. If you recall, there is a small airscoop on the fuselage just forward of the cockpit that provided ram air for the cockpit ventilation system. The intake did have a heavy wire screen to protect it from anything but a direct hit. The efficacy of Murphy's Law again prevailed as it triumphed over the laws of chance. Fortunately, the only casualty (besides my stained skivvies!) was one of the coolant lines. An

Shot down in a pinball

When I departed Kingman Army Air Field in early April of 1945, it was with a lighthearted feeling of relief. I was happy but my wife wasn't enjoying things too much. I was on my way to combat at long last. Hooray and hallelujah! My assignment was Lincoln Army Air Field, Nebraska, at that time the Air Force distribution center for flying personnel destined for combat theaters. My friends and I had heard of the forthcoming frangible bullet program and had flown indoctrination flights in the target aircraft, but about twenty of us were gone before the firing missions began. We little dreamed then that we would be actively participating in the second pinball phase.

Our stay at Lincoln was short-lived; the war in Europe came to an end in May and to accommodate the numerous flying officers waiting at Atlantic ports of embarkation, we were summarily removed from Lincoln to make room for them. It was another low blow to all of us, especially when we learned that we were returning to a Flying Training Command flexible gunnery school, in our case, Las Vegas, Nevada, and later to Indian Springs, the fighter sub-base about thirty miles north of the main airfield.

The welcoming address by the commanding officer at Indian Springs contained very little about the anticipated frangible bullet missions and a great deal about the moral pitfalls awaiting us in the nearby sin capital of Las Vegas. This was May and it was well into June before we received our first briefing on pinball missions.

I don't recall being particularly concerned about our forthcoming duties. We knew the preliminary phase of the program had been conducted during the month of April at all of the flexible gunnery schools and they had been called off (we were told) in order to convert to B-29 gunnery training. I find in my Form Five what appears to be my first pinball mission on June 23 with pinball flights continuing through July. I departed Indian Springs on emergency leave August 1 and the program was over when I returned later in the month.

I flew a lot of missions in those five weeks and I found them to be a real and fascinating challenge. They were considerably different, in many respects, from the camera missions we had flown with the P-39s and P-63s. I noticed right away that the reduced performance of the RP manifested itself in the way I was forced to fly the curve of pursuit. It was practically full throttle all the time; otherwise it would have taken too long to reposition following a pass. It must also be remembered that the speed of the bombers had been reduced in the very beginning, a mandatory requirement to compensate for the different frangible bullet ballistics.

Also, for obvious reasons, one fighter was assigned to a single bomber. They were all B-24s at Las Vegas, configured with a variation of B-29 sights, we were told, and with a single .30 caliber machine gun mounted in the waist. Watching smoke wisping from that gun as I came in on a pass was attention-getting, believe me. We were not permitted to cross under the bomber so we had to continue our turn, and this exposed the unarmored belly of the RP as we moved away. This was a critical moment in the breakaway as I was to learn. It was only when the gunner kept firing after the break that there was reason for concern. This happened more than once and I always notified the bomber pilot, in no uncertain terms, of the breach of safety procedures.

Many of the wartime student gunners maintain they never hit the target airplane. I was hit, many times. I remember well the shuddering impact of a frangible slug striking the windshield, leaving a visible puff of blue dust on the glass surface. The sound was like someone hitting the aircraft with a heavy hammer. I also remember the cockpit counter revolving like mad on occasion. I knew I was being hit, notwithstanding the history of counter malfunctions. I always found visual confirmation upon landing and examining the aircraft surfaces.

The pinball program came to an end shortly after the fifth RP had been shot down within a week in the vicinity of Indian Springs, not including the one back in April. Rumor had it that the reason frangible bullet missions had been scrubbed throughout Training Command was because of these losses. One of them resulted in a fatality when friend and companion attempted to stretch his glide into one of the many dry lakes dotting the Nevada landscape. He had received a hit in a radiator and, while this is the only known tragedy in the pinball program to my knowledge, I remember it had a most sobering effect on all of us.

There was a lot of talk about the first pinball downed back in April, the one where the pilot temporarily passed out from cockpit fumes and broke a leg bailing out, as described in the Preface. If he had been on oxygen at the time he probably would have had presence of mind to attempt a forced landing. We'll never know, of course, but it did result in a safety rule that stood some of us in good stead. At the time I flew pinball missions, we were admonished to fly with oxygen mask on at all times. When I experienced my moment of truth in the final week of July, coolant fumes entering the cockpit resulted in no physical impairment at all.

I was hit on the break at the end of one of my initial passes on this mission. I had just observed the student firing as I pulled away and I was making another complaint to the bomber pilot when he informed me, in return, that I was trailing what appeared to be smoke. Right then I knew what had happened. I kept my eyes on the coolant and oil temperature gauges as I broke away and headed back to Indian Springs. Pretty soon (it must have been only seconds later) I saw the coolant needle start to creep upward and, without further ado, I cut my engine. Fortunately, I was then directly over a large, dry lake and I set up a circular pattern for a forced landing.

I had no problem getting in dead stick, keeping a little extra airspeed just to be safe. I made it, gear down and with lots of room to spare. Deplaning on the cracked, hard mud surface of the old lake bed, I examined my aircraft and found a jagged, angled hole on the bottom of the wing root from which ethylene glycol still dripped. It seems like all the aircraft in the vicinity were echoing my "Mayday" call while I was descending, and it wasn't long before I was picked up and returned to home base.

I really didn't believe I could accomplish anything at all in the form of remedial action, but I was determined to try. Firing on the break had become too prevalent, to my way of thinking, and I was convinced the subject should be made a matter of utmost concern to all people involved. After my debriefing that day, I asked for and was granted permission to fly down to the main base and see if I could at least track down the culprit and his supervisor. I had the number of the offending bomber, of course, but even with this positive identification, all I received at Las Vegas was a runaround. A typical example, you might say, of the lack of cooperation that existed between bomber and fighter crews in that day and age.

We heard about the new RP-63s coming off the Bell assembly line and most of us were looking forward to flying them. They were reputed to be superior performers with more protection for the pilot. We were also hoping something constructive had been accomplished by the aircraft engineers to eliminate the rash of accidents caused by damage to the cooling systems. Most of the pilots I knew felt that the pinball program, despite its shortcomings and inherent dangers, was the training device of the future. I was sorry to witness its sudden demise, although the prospects of early separation from the service were attractive indeed. By October, I was on my way home, only to be recalled nearly five years later early in the Korean conflict.

Pinballs remained, over the years, a nostalgic memory to me, rekindled lately by numerous contacts with those who also participated in this most challenging and, in many ways, most fascinating experiment in the annals of aerial gunnery training.

immediate return to base saved the day before the engine froze from lack of coolant.

"As for the lessons learned from my duty at Yuma, I found out if I didn't want to get hit, all I had to do was hold some rudder during the pass and slide the ball out of the center of the race. As far as I was concerned, that constituted cheating and except for a little experimenting with it, I always tried to give them a well-coordinated pass."

There were incidents aplenty, as Ed Wakeland will attest. Here he tells how Harlingen school officials went about instilling confidence in some of the skeptical target pilots: "The brass arranged to get a plane set up on the gunnery range. All had a chance to try and penetrate the armor . . . to no avail. The windshield and canopy doors were the favorite targets, but they were very thick and shatter proof. No luck."

After checking out it wasn't long before all the qualified pilots were flying pinball missions. Wakeland remembers one of his friends who had a very close call: "He was asked to check the fuel cap on one of the B-24s, so he flew in close and told the B-24 pilot it was okay. Then he noticed the gunner in the waist was blasting away at him—so he peeled off. Unfortunately, one of the frangibles got into an air intake and knocked out his oil radiator. He managed to make an emergency landing at the base, even with the cockpit full of smoke. He ejected the left door and could see well enough to get stopped and get out with no harm. All of the pinballs were grounded and, as far as I know, flew no more passes at the B-24s."

Karl Edmondson also experienced some of the pinball hazards flying out of Laredo. He received a cracked windshield which, according to most, was very unusual. Edmondson tells about his experience:

"At the time I got the cracked windshield, I had just rolled into the pursuit curve when a waist gunner in the B-24 cut loose. His first burst was very accurate and the crack appeared. I just kept rolling till I was inverted and dropped away as fast as possible. I called the B-24 and told him what had happened and suggested in rather firm language they return to base and change the bullet composition. I acted strictly on reflex and don't recall hearing a noise or seeing the bullet hit. One second it was not there and the next second it was. Also on landing I found a few slight dents I don't think were there before the flight." Ed Arbogast, who was stationed at Laredo, verifies Edmondson's story. Arbogast remembers the RP-63 with the cracked windshield, a graphic reminder that frangible ammunition was, indeed, powerful enough to cause damage.

Edmondson doesn't recall a pinball being shot down but recalls a number forced to return to base because of minor damage. He tells about one or two that came back with bullet holes in the propeller. (This must have been caused by regular ammunition. Frangibles would not penetrate a prop blade and it's very unlikely they would cause the bulletproof glass in an RP-63 windshield to crack.) Edmondson maintains you could tell when a prop was damaged because of the sound of the prop whistling on final approach.

Merlyn Franck witnessed some of the early RP-63 tests at Laredo and was privileged to fly the original pinball. Franck says Laredo had a very aggressive program, and indeed it did. This Texas base was the center for frangible bullet mission tests, and many of the training improvements originated there. Franck recalls one close call experienced by a Laredo fighter pilot who received a hit "right at the point (where) the door and door frame met." Some of the tiny pieces of the bullet came through and struck the pilot in the face. Franck says the flyer panicked and declared an emergency, thinking he had been shot. It turned out he had not been injured and came out of the incident with only small dust smudges on his face.

Richard Lake knows what it's like to be shot down. As he tells it, "Nothing can get your attention quicker than the impact of a frangible bullet on the windscreen." Lake was stationed at Harlingen during the pinball program and he had the "dubious distinction of being shot down over the US and by my own kind." The incident is still fresh in his mind. "On July 12, 1945," he recalls, "I was flying a mission about forty miles from the Harlingen sub-base of Laguna-Madre, when the B-24 pilot called me and told me I was streaming something white behind. I switched tanks, thinking I was siphoning off the full tank. When I advanced the throttle to get back into position, the Allison began to make strange sounds and all the gauges headed for the red. At that point I knew what 'something white' meant."

Lake went through his emergency procedures, including oil and coolant shutters full open, mixture full rich, and priming every thirty seconds or so, but about forty miles later the engine froze. "I made it to the runway," he goes on, "but didn't have enough airspeed to flare. The nose gear snapped and we came sliding to a halt on the main gear and two prop blades. Investigation revealed I had taken a hit in the left air intake and a coolant radiator seam was split on that side. The next day the Good Lord decided I was more suited for the Ferry Command and I agreed."

Pilots soon learned that pinball missions could be a deadly serious business, but there was still a certain amount of horseplay. Target pilots liked to taunt the ineffective student gunners; conversely, gunnery instructors frequently complained about poor fighter passes. Charles Pierce remembers the P-63 pilot who, after making a number of passes without a hit, pulled up on the right wing of his bomber and, in jest, asked the gunner if he could "hit me now!" The gunner obliged and the fighter pilot, forgetting that frangible ammunition could be quite lethal at such short range, found himself in a veritable hailstorm of .30 caliber bullets. Pierce can't recall the extent of damage to the pinball but it definitely provided a lesson one fighter pilot would not soon forget.

There were numerous instances of pinballs flying formation with the firing aircraft. Clyde W. Myers was a B-17 pilot stationed at Yuma in the summer of 1945. Myers had a unique way of coordinating bomber and fighter crew activities. This is how he explains it:

"Before we would fly, I would have the fighter pilot talk to the student gunners. [This was possible where bombers and fighters operated out of the same base. At most stations, this was not the case.] Hits were fifteen to twenty per 1,000 rounds but the frangible bullet coming out of the barrel had a habit of taking off in different directions. [No proof of this.] The pinball pilot would make a pursuit curve from above, slanting down toward the waist gunner. Our fighter pilots could come extremely close in order to get hits. At the end of the firing range, the pinball would fly formation. At this time, if a student decided to shoot, a hit would be in an unarmored area. A comment, such as 'gunner, do not fire' would cause an immediate peel off of the fighter. One pinball did get a bullet in the cooling system and had to make a forced landing in the desert.

"It did give the gunnery students a chance to fire a waist machine gun with live ammunition at an attacking fighter aircraft," Myers concludes, joining a host of others who appreciated the new training program.

Marcus Galyear spent a tour of duty as communications officer at Buckingham in 1945. He maintains that hits, especially during the trial phase, were few and far between. About the only time he remembers the hit counters working was when someone would tap the RP with a hammer.

E. R. (Bud) McCafferty relates some interesting sidelights of the pinball period. "I graduated in Class 44-I from Williams Army Air Field on Dec. 23, 1944," McCafferty writes. "We were immediately told there was no further need for fighter pilots, that we would become B-17 copilots. There was some talk of the

The coolant system of a P-63C. All Bell fighters were similarly configured. Note twin radiators (5) located in wing roots and expansion tank (2). Ram air was directed to radiators by means of ducts leading from air intake in wing root. Author's collection

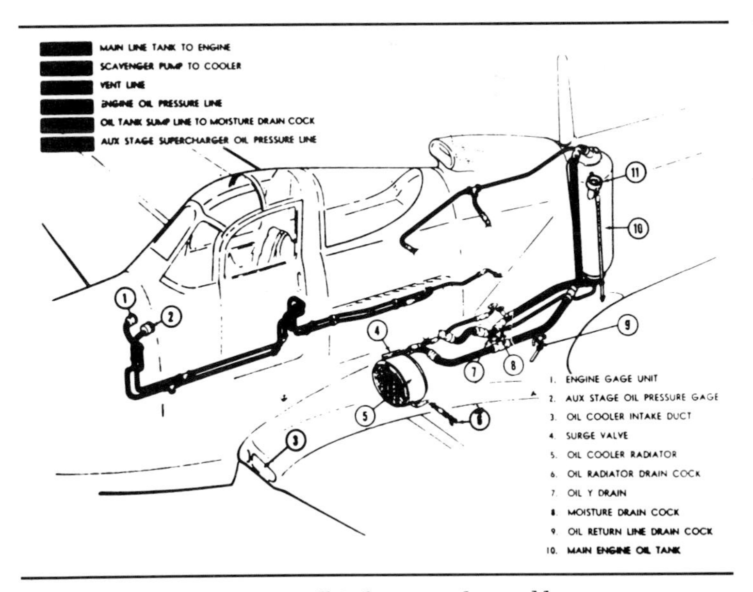

The oil cooling radiator on Bell fighters was located between coolant radiators in the bottom of the fuselage. Oil radiator shared cooling air with coolant radiators from common duct. Author's collection

whole class joining the Luftwaffe. What the hell! *They* needed fighter pilots. But nothing came of that, of course.

"So some of us went to Yuma, a flexible gunnery school among other things. Apparently they were sort of 'killing two stones with one bird'—that is, conducting B-17 copilot training in the front of the airplane, flexible gunnery in the rear. This was in January and February of 1945. They were towing targets with B-25s and Martin B-26s [AT-23s] and making approaches for the waist gunners with RP-63s. [The pinball program did not start until April.] It was a bit of a frightening thing the first time I sat there straight and level and watched that fighter come in on a smooth curve without breaking off until he was *close!* But we got used to that. It seemed rather infrequent that we saw any indications of hits. The rumor was it was very unusual for the system on the RP-63 to work properly, even if those students did hit it.

"I remember two incidents in particular while I was at Yuma. A student shot an engine off a B-25 while they were going by with the sleeve. The B-25 pilots were waiting for the B-17 when it landed, ready to take personal charge of said student. They were forcibly prevented from doing so.

"The other one I witnessed from in front of the operations shack. The RP-63s all carried a centerline drop tank. [This was an unusual configuration, except for ferry flights. This incident probably involved a pinball being delivered to Yuma.] This particular pilot neglected to drop his gear and landed on the drop tank instead. He skated down the runway with a hell of a big fire right behind him. The airplane slid to a stop more or less in front of the ops shack. The door flew open, the pilot leaped out, jumped off the wing and ran about fifty feet away, slammed his chute down on the asphalt, sat on it and watched the airplane burn until the firemen put the fire out. I was shipped out shortly thereafter and never heard what may have befallen the pilot, poor guy."

John Behrens tells of some of the mechanical damage inflicted on RPs: "I recall there were several spare doors because the glass had a tendency to crack. Those super-thick windows didn't roll down like the regular ones. The cracking seemed to be induced while taxiing with the doors propped open. So, after we ran out of spares at Indian Springs in a very short time, some wise guy ordered us to taxi with the doors closed . . . I think that's how they invented the steam cabinet. All that—*and gloves and oxygen mask too!*

"The mask was required after we lost a pinball that suffered a one-in-a-million shot into the oil lines somewhere. Smoke came up into the cockpit and the pilot hit the panic button and bailed out . . . and with all those nice dry lakes all over the place! And, of course, a high g-force turn or a hard landing could really run up the score on the counter in the cockpit."

Barrie Davis was a fighter pilot at Indian Springs. He witnessed some of the more serious incidents. "On at least two occasions [more like six], RP-63s were shot down by frangible bullets," Davis maintains. "They (the bullets) entered the radiator air intakes at the leading edge of the wing, penetrated the radiator and permitted the coolant to escape. Overheated engines don't run long and so planes bellied in on the desert. They usually suffered surprisingly little damage. [Most of the pinballs shot down at Indian Springs landed gear down on dry lakes.]

"When gunners were about to graduate, they were supposed to achieve a certain number of hits to pass their final test. Gunners had all sorts of problems achieving acceptable scores, but the fault was not ours. If we knew a class was near graduation, some of us would occasionally fly fairly close formation with the B-24s to make easy targets. [That was really asking for it. I can't recall anyone at Indian Springs taking that kind of risk.]

"I've heard pilots mention hearing bullets striking their planes. I never heard anything I thought was a bullet strike. Since counters in the cockpit seldom worked, we did not know how skilled the gunners were until we landed and visually counted the strikes. I do know that when we compared the number of passes we made at the bombers with the number of hits made on our target planes, we had great confidence in the superiority of fighters over bombers."

Carl Weaver also remembers the poor scores tallied by gunnery students and the efforts made to inflate them at Kingman. "For both camera and frangible bullet missions," Weaver says, "we fighter pilots were directed to make it as easy as possible for the gunners. We used the high-side approach with a shallow curve of pursuit, closing to within about 200 feet and ten to fifteen degrees angle-off. To my knowledge, I was never hit on my two pinball flights. We made about fifteen passes per mission. My totalizers (counters) never registered. However, there were no elaborate debriefings in those times, so I don't know if the gunners ever lit up my nose."

Wilbur Bailey, a fighter squadron commanding officer in 1945 at Laguna Madre, Harlingen's sub-base, provides some interesting information on typical flight line activities, and a not-so-typical incident that occurred in the performance of his job. This is his story:

"With roster in hand I checked off those in attendance. The usual bridge game was in progress in the ready room with cribbage on the side. I read off the names of those who should be there but were not. I received verbal reports from anyone who had knowledge of the whereabouts of the missing pilots. Excuses for nonattendance were accepted without question. After all, weren't we all combat returnees and officers and gentlemen by act of Congress?

"I read off missions of the day and placed them on the schedule board. First priority for flight went to pilots who needed time for flight pay (four hours per month). Soon I had a pilot assigned for each mission, whether frangible or camera firing. We flew RP-63s for frangible and P-63s for camera missions.

"By noon the morning missions had been flown and the pilots were drifting off to mess or home as the case might be. The p.m. group would not show up until between 1:15 and 1:30. All went well until the last mission of the afternoon when I found that the assigned pilot, who had been called to the main base, had not returned. This was a frequent occurrence, especially on Friday afternoons when people tended to drift away early. I always stood in for them and usually by the month's end, had more flight time than most of my charges.

"I drew my chute and gear from the chute trailer on the line, cranked up one of my RPs and met my B-24 on the range out over the gulf. The waist gunners fired high without many recorded hits and a frontal pass that was repeated so quickly the gunners did not have a chance to fire. Indeed, on the first pass, no one on the B-24 even saw me go by. The closing speed was about 450-500 mph and I went under the B-24 with a clearance of thirty to forty feet. [This frontal pass is surprising. At Las Vegas we were told they were strictly forbidden at all training bases. This had to have been a special mission using nose guns, which I never knew about.]

"The B-24 radioed they had finished firing and I could return to base. I turned for home, letting down from nine thousand. I noticed a flock of sheep (white, puffy clouds) had moved over the base and into the Laguna Madre and Padre Islands. They were pretty, lying there with their cooling shade underneath. I reduced power and dove for the high key, 1,500 feet over the center of the active runway. As I turned on my downwind, I noticed the 'sheep' were on a pool table (all cloud bases at the same altitude) at about 400 feet. I rolled onto base leg and cut power, lowered gear and made my old GUMP cockpit check from training days (gas, undercarriage, mixture and propeller). I lined up on the approach, dropped full flaps and figured touchdown on the runway numbers.

"Tower gave me 'clear to land' but just as I descended below the base of the 'sheep,' everything went white! My super-cooled airplane had condensed fog on the outside of all my cockpit windows. I was immediately on instrument conditions—needle, ball and airspeed. Applying cruise power, I held the airspeed constant at 120-130 mph, and eased back on the stick until the altimeter started up. I uncaged my gyros and things began looking better. I 'milked' up some flap and increased airspeed.

"Just as suddenly as it appeared, the fog became water droplets and ran off the cockpit windows in streaks. I found myself above the sheep again, safe and sound. I flew until the windows warmed up, then landed without further incident.

"The tower personnel thought the event hilarious. They said the plane was about to land, then with a nose-down attitude flew straight down the runway at about 50 feet and out of sight. I was happy I could laugh with them."

Pilots aren't the only ones with memories of the frangible bullet program. Gunners, both instructors and students, had definite opinions of the pinball missions and they don't all coincide. Ira George was a believer. He participated in the pinball program at Buckingham in the spring of 1945, a member of the first formal B-29 gunnery training class. "Prior to 1945," George recalls, "gunners for the B-29 units were either prior combat-experienced flexible turret gunners or were graduates of other flexible gunnery schools. To the best of my knowledge, the frangible training was also the first available in the Air Force. According to my instructors, they were the first to introduce the program into formal training schedules. [Pinball training was introduced simultaneously at all flexible gunnery schools.]

"This class was also the first in which the gunners were assigned to crews composed of a computer control gunner specialist, an armament specialist, an aircraft mechanic specialist and a tail gunner (no specialty), all of whom went through gunnery training together. We also went on to OTU together and wound up overseas on the same crew. Prior to this, flexible gunners, like myself, were trained and sent overseas to repo depots (replacement depots) or centers. From there they were assigned to a group, thence to a squadron, and ultimately to a crew.

"Back to flexible gunnery. Each crew in my class was given one flight in a B-24 equipped with a .30 caliber machine gun and frangible bullets. We were flown out over the Everglades and were met (intercepted) by an orange-colored RP-63. Each member was allowed to fire at him during two passes. Being tail gunner, I was last, but according to the pilot and instructors, the first to ever register hits.

"We fired on the two passes from the right waist position. I only got to fire on one pass, but I got hits. As I recall, it was an old B-24 with modified windows over the waist positions. That is, you couldn't open the windows. There was also a modified gun mount in the center of the right plexiglass window. It was an old .50 caliber gun mount changed over to hold a .30 caliber machine gun. We got a strip of twenty rounds for each pass and the RP-63 flew an early World War II pursuit curve, breaking down and away toward the tail.

"This kind of pursuit curve attack had been standard in the ETO against the B-17s . . . when the Germans had air supremacy, not necessarily superiority, over Europe. The standard newsreel fare demonstrating the 'attack against Fortress Europa'... (we all) have seen many times. The Me(Bf)109 is on a curve of pursuit attack and virtually sticks his nose into the waist gunner's face before breaking away. This kind of attack ended in 1943 when our bombers got their little friends (escort fighters). After that, the attacks usually came from front, on a fly-through, or a fly-past attack (across the formations). 'Get the hell in and out' became the German motto.

"The sight used for frangible training was the standard rad-ring. Even the B-29 had a hard time lugging around the remote control computer under the floor boards between the waist gunners. One of the major reasons why Curt LeMay, then commanding general of the 20th Air Force, stripped his B-29s of all turrets and guns (except for the tail gunner who had to revert to the old rad-ring sighting by a special fix in the sight) was to reduce weight, thus increasing the aircraft's bomb-carrying capacity."

Many of the student gunners had little faith in the frangible bullet concept and can't remember any hits on the target aircraft at all. Erroll Williams attended gunnery school at Buckingham and he, too, was trained to become a B-29 gunner. "All of our flying training was conducted in B-24s," he writes, "some of which had been converted with B-29 turrets. However, for the frangible bullet program we fired pedestal-mounted .30 caliber machine guns from the waist position. As I recall, the gunsight was a rather crude reticle type without lead computing capability. I only recall firing at RP-63s on two or three flights and I doubt any of us on those flights had any hits.

"The RP-63s were supposed to be equipped with a counter to register hits. They flew a pursuit curve attack to expose only the frontal area. I vividly remember on the very first pass, we were not ready to fire but the target pilot radioed our pilot we had twenty hits. So much for the accuracy of the counter. As for the pinball's nose which was supposed to light up when hits were made, I don't know if this was truth or fiction. I never saw one light up. It was also reported that an RP had been shot down, but I was never able to confirm this."

Another Buckingham Field student during this period was Harry J. Byer. He recalls very little of the pinball program that could be termed successful. He, too, was pursuing B-29 gunnery training and remembers that B-24s were fitted with B-29 gunsights. "The waist windows were left open," Byer remembers, "and each window had a swivel-mounted, hand-held .30 caliber gun. We fired at bright orange RP-63s out of Naples, Florida. It was explained to us that the reason for using .30 caliber instead of .50 caliber was the fact that frangibles couldn't stand the muzzle velocity of the .50s. [Neither could the target planes.]

"The gunnery range was in the Everglades. We usually flew at 6,000 feet while a single pinball made conventional high-side passes, rolling in about two o'clock and terminating a pursuit curve at around four o'clock. The bomber pilot cleared us to fire and stop by interphone. At the end of each pass, the fighter pilot would call off the number of hits. The majority of the time it was negative, accompanied by some sporty, taunting language. The firing was highly ineffective due to the guns continually jamming and using a ring and post sight without any tracers. As a result, you hadn't the faintest idea where your fire was going."

Archie P. Callahan was assigned to the Central Instructors School at Laredo after completing his combat tours. He fired his first frangible bullets in August of 1945. "I fired a .30 caliber hand-held machine gun from the waist of a B-17 as an RP-63 made a pass at us," he recalls. "I had a 'bird' colonel giving me instructions. He told me to open fire at 600 yards, but to stop when the fighter closed to 300 yards. They were not sure the bullets would disintegrate as planned. I was getting good hits when the target plane broke off and dove away. I remember the colonel saying, 'I hope you didn't shoot him down for real.' I met the pilot later and he said 'Damn, I was getting peppered!'"

Donald E. Matthews was one of the doubters. He was a gunnery student at Tyndall in the spring of 1945 when he participated in pinball missions. "I myself did not hit an RP," he maintains, "and I don't recall anyone from my class who did. The bullet was too light to be effective. We used it once on a tow target and the bullets went through the target sideways. As students we did not consider it an effective program."

Harold Ericsson was a bombardier/navigator during the last year of the war and took gunnery training at Harlingen and Las Vegas. He derived little benefit from the program, but readily admits it provided training that could have been of real value.

"I was a member of the first B-29 class at Las Vegas," Ericsson recalls, "and we didn't have much to do. The course wasn't nearly as well structured as at Harlingen. We had lectures on the frangible bullet, I remember, and were told they had developed it for both the .30 and .50 calibers but that they had some trouble with the .50 caliber and we would only use the .30. [Many false reports and rumors were widespread at this time. The .50 caliber was never considered for frangible bullet training.]

"As far as training with frangible bullets is concerned, I didn't make too many of those (missions), maybe a couple. All of the firing was with hand-held waist guns from a B-24 and we used just plain iron sights. I don't believe I ever hit anything with that thing. I never had anybody tell me I did, anyway.

"I believe one member of our class, Flight Officer Paul C. Farst, shot an RP-63 down. Paul was a friend of mine and although I wasn't on the flight, I heard about it from Paul and it appeared to be authentic. He fired a burst and scored hits on the target's oil cooler. According to the report, the B-24 pilot notified the target plane's pilot he was streaming something behind his aircraft and got an uppity response, something like 'You fly your airplane and I'll take care of mine!' Well, the guy got so many fumes in his cockpit he had to bail out and I hear he broke a leg." (This is the subject of the Preface.)

The discussions and arguments continue and there will never be consensus among the people involved. A better criterion of the value of the frangible bullet program lies in the evaluation conducted by higher headquarters. There is little doubt the pinball would have become the primary flexible gunnery training tool had the war continued much longer. Improvements were contemplated and actually in production at the end of the Training Command program, improvements which would have contributed significantly to the overall value of frangible bullet training. Regardless of the end result, the active participants retain memories, some good, some bad, that will remain forever.

After the war

11

For all intents and purposes, flexible gunnery training on a coordinated, Air Force-wide basis, ended with the cessation of hostilities late in 1945. It continued in Strategic Air Command for awhile, but Training Command proceeded immediately to close or change the mission of the seven airfields originally dedicated to teaching aerial gunners how to handle machine guns in combat.

A new era was dawning and top-level military planners were quick to foretell the effect newly developed jet aircraft would have on aerial combat tactics. It was a whole new ball game, as Ira George tells us. George completed a full tour with the Air Force and remembers some later postwar incidents that involved him. He recalls with justifiable pride that he was the first gunner to shoot down a target drone using the B-29 remote sighting system.

George also had considerable practice firing camera guns against jets when he "shot" one down while serving with the Strategic Air Command. This occurred during one of SAC's intrusion exercises against the San Diego Air Defense System when the Navy scrambled three jet fighters against the attacking force. Using only the old rad-ring mode, George was fortunate in getting one sure "kill" and "damage" to another. However, it was finally determined during this test that normally a gunner just couldn't track fast enough to keep his guns aligned on a speeding jet aircraft with any degree of consistency.

There are instances of jets downed during World War II, mostly by happenstance, however. Ed Arbogast tells of a master sergeant named Muehlenberg who supposedly shot down the first Me 163 by firing way ahead of the speeding aircraft and tracking backwards, allowing the rocket fighter to fly into his cone of fire. This didn't happen too often.

Strangely enough, despite the sudden cessation of the pinball program in Air Training Command, frangible bullet training continued in SAC at three locations. During this time the RP-63G, the newly configured pinball upon which the Air Force had placed such high hopes, made its only appearance in the role for which it was developed. Kemper W. Baker probably flew the last G model into Hill Army Air Field at Ogden, Utah, for retirement, subsequent to its short-lived program at Alamogordo, New Mexico. "As I remember," Baker writes, "we opened Alamogordo to set up a gunnery school in 1945 using the frangible bullet concept. It was the period immediately following the severe military reductions by Secretary of Defense Louis Johnson under President Truman. Because of the cuts, our project/school was short lived."

Alamogordo was a follow-up to the initial SAC pinball program located at Pueblo, Colorado, for a short time. Orlando C. Asper participated in this early phase and he tells about some of his experiences:

"I was aircraft commander of a B-29 crew, TDY from Fairmont, Nebraska, on this frangible bullet program at Pueblo. The program lasted for some three months starting in August of 1945. The B-29 was No. 1706, mothballed shortly thereafter and 'rescued' in 1951 or 1952. I later flew the same aircraft over Korea in early 1953. The TDY group from Fairmont included ten maintenance personnel.

"We usually tried to fly two 2½ hour missions each day, five days a week. We always flew straight and level at 180 mph with the pinballs coming in at various angles. The B-29 guns and turrets were modified from .50 to .30 caliber for the frangible bullets. The B-29 crew fired on the targets beginning at 600 yards and shutting down at 200 yards. We never shot a pinball

The B-29 was a mainstay of the Strategic Air Command for a time after the cessation of hostilities in 1945. Final pinball missions were flown against this bomber with the RP-63G. Ernest R. McDowell

Alamogordo, New Mexico, was the site of the final pinball missions. Strategic Air Command continued training with B-29s and RP-63Gs. Photo shows part of the organization at Alamogordo, officers in back, enlisted men front two rows. The tail surfaces of a pinball can be seen between number one and two B-29 engines. Norman Stiver

down, but we severely damaged windshields and control surfaces on several occasions."

There were some lighthearted moments along with the serious business of firing live ammunition at friendly aircraft. It was an interesting period for Asper. "On one occasion," he recalls, "I called for landing instructions for one B-29 and five pinballs! The landing was a 360-degree overhead approach and with power cut back on numbers one and two engines, the B-29 circled tightly and landed with five 'chicks' in tow. Needless to say, I was chided by the base ops officer."

N. W. (Norm) Stiver was at Alamogordo, and he left a detailed, chronological summary of the SAC frangible bullet training project. Most of it is of a personal nature, outlining his day-to-day activities, and it confirms the relocation of the training unit from Pueblo in the early part of 1946 to Tarrant Field, Fort Worth, Texas, and subsequently to Alamogordo in the summer. Stiver says the Alamogordo program was scheduled to last three years. However, the whole thing came to an end because of a lack of funds after a relatively short period of time.

With SAC's final effort, pinball training at long last was over; by the end of 1947 all RP-63s in the Air Force inventory had been mothballed. But the frangible concept itself would not die. Over the years there have been various attempts to resurrect the theory and put it to practical use. As early as 1946, a 30 mm frangible projectile was developed and tested on ground gunnery ranges, in an attempt to eliminate accidents caused by bullet ricochet during ground strafing runs by jet aircraft. This projectile represented quite a departure from the original .30 caliber ammunition used in the pinball program. It was much larger, of course. The outer body was made of molded plastic while the inner body consisted of steel washers, or platelets. When the relatively weak plastic skin ruptured on impact, the platelets would scatter. Due to their relatively low energy and high drag factor, the washers could not travel as far as a regular, deflected bullet. Tests were made but the concept, as near as can be determined, was never implemented as part of any accepted gunnery training mission.

The World War II system of flexible gunnery defense on aerial missions lasted only a short time after the conflict ended. The B-29 had already pioneered remote gun aiming and firing, and the newer, more sophisticated jet aircraft eschewed the now antiquated

After the war, this RP-63 was put on permanent display at Lackland AFB. The photo was taken in January 1980, and the plane is painted in bright-orange pinball colors. Ken Dowd

methods entirely. Recognizing that jet-powered bombers could fly almost as fast as fighters, there was no longer a need to provide lateral or forward defensive armament. It was quickly ascertained that for a fighter to assume a position sufficiently ahead of its target to make a pursuit or beam attack, the time element required was enough alone to make this type of attack prohibitive.

New offensive weapons systems rely almost entirely on missiles, although the rapid-fire Gatling 20 mm cannon is still in use. However, it is a fixed weapon and inflexible, even in the C-47 gunbus airplanes used for ground strafing in Vietnam. The B-52, still our most numerous long-range bomber—it has been in the Air Force inventory more years than crews care to contemplate—is protected only by 20 mm guns located in

This photo show Lackland's RP-63 as it is today—stripped of its orange paint. Merlin Franck

the tail, guarding only against attacks from the rear. Added to this, the advent of microchip technology has made the lightweight computer an airborne necessity, relegating the gunner to an even less important or nonexistent role. The B-1 bomber, now on active operational duty, is the last word in offensive aerial weaponry and it contains no visible sign of defensive armament.

For many years the flexible gunner was an important, even necessary part of each and every bomber crew. That the frangible bullet program, with its spectacular pinballs, was once an important part of our national defense is a matter of pride to those who played a part in this unique, long-remembered training effort.

Appendix A

Division 2, National Defense Research Committee
of the
Office of Scientific Research and Development

The frangible bullet for use in aerial gunnery training

Final Report

General Summary

The investigations presented in this report are the result of an attempt to find a solution to the problem of training aerial gunners by having them fire live ammunition at an attacking pursuit airplane, thus simulating the conditions of combat to a close degree. It was hoped a bullet could be found that would be able to withstand the stresses in the firing process but be defeated by relatively light armor and therefore be suitable for use in a training device.

A. Bullet

In view of preliminary tests reported elsewhere, it seemed possible that a plastic bullet filled with a dense material might have the desired qualities. Accordingly, arrangements were made with the Bakelite Corporation to supply molded materials for fabrication into bullets which were then tested for their suitability. The tests included measurement of the limit impact velocity of the bullets against a given target metal, their ability to withstand loading and firing, and their stability in flight. It was decided that a composition designated as Bakelite RD-42-93 was the most promising, and it was therefore adopted for production of a frangible bullet, subsequently called the T44 bullet by the Ordnance Department. The bullet produced from the plastic is approximately the same shape as the caliber .30 M2 ball bullet, weighs 6.95 plus or minus 0.11, gm (107, plus or minus 1.5, grains), and has a density d_{25} of 6.93, plus or minus 0.08, gm/ml. The ballistic tables for the bullet were determined by the Aberdeen Proving Ground, and the ballistic coefficient on the basis of the T44 Sciacci functions was found to be 0.163. The bullet may be fired through a Springfield rifle or caliber .30 Browning AC M2 machine gun with a muzzle velocity as high as 2400 ft/sec without showing signs of breakup or damage. The limit impact velocity of the T44 bullet against ¼-in. 24ST dural armor plate is 1750, plus or minus 20, ft./sec. in comparison with 1390, plus or minus 20, ft./sec. for a .30 caliber bullet reduced to the mass of a T44 bullet. It was decided on the basis of the requirements for pilot safety involved and the protection which could be afforded by the permissible weight of armor on the fighter plane that a muzzle velocity of 1360 ft./sec. was allowable for the T44 bullet. This gives ballistic performance such that a sight could be adjusted so that the leads on a reticle-diameter basis required of a student gunner could be made practically identical with those required in combat with caliber .50 ammunition. The maximum practical firing range for the T44 bullet, as now in use, is about 700 yd. and maximum contact range is about 600 yd.

A number of variables in the production and use of the frangible bullets have been studied. It has been determined that variations in the lead powder do not produce significant variations in the limit impact velocity of the bullets and that considerable variation is possible in the time, temperature, and pressure factors affecting the cure during the molding process, without appreciably affecting the resulting bullet. Similarly, no significant change occurs in finished bullets subjected to accelerated aging by heat or cold treatment. No difference was found in the limit impact velocity of bullets fired at room temperature and at -68° against armor at room temperature.

On impact against light armor the frangible bullet breaks into fine particles. Photographs made with an Eastman high-speed movie camera show that the bullet disintegrates within 0.19 millisecond upon impact against dural armor of about 1300 ft./sec.

B. Armor

Along with experiments to determine a bullet suitable for air-to-air firing, certain other problems associated with use of the bullet came within the scope of this project. One of these was the ability of armor to different types to withstand impact of the frangible bullet. This was investigated with a view of determining the type and thickness of armor necessary to use in armoring a plane to protect the pilot and essential engine parts. Different armor plates were compared on the basis of their limit impact velocity. Limit impact velocities were obtained for all plates for shots fired at normal incidence (90°), and, in some cases, at lower angles of incidence since some parts of the target plane need only to be protected from hits by bullets at an angle of 45° or less.

Three general types of armor were studied. First, dural armor plate of various types and thicknesses (1/16, 3/32, 1/8, 3/16, 1/4, 5/16, 3/8, 1/2, and 3/4-in.); steel armor manufactured by the Jessop Steel Company (thicknesses of 3/32, 1/8, 5/32, and 3/15-in.); and third, Doron, which consists of laminated layers of loosely woven fiber glass bonded with plastic (thicknesses of 8/86, 13/64, and 26/64-in.).

Of the dural plates tested, Alcoa 24ST and Reynolds .301T were found to be the only types that could be used efficiently in armoring a target plane in terms of protection afforded and weight of metal. As might be expected, bare 24ST dural plate is superior to Alclad plate of equal thickness. It was also found that, within limits, higher-strength materials, as measured by static testing procedures, are superior to those of lower strength. Preliminary tests indicate that multiple thickness armor is slightly less effective than a single sheet of comparable thickness. Low temperatures (-50°C) increases the limit impact velocity of $\frac{1}{4}$-in. 24ST dural by about 50 ft./sec., although the armor appears to become somewhat more brittle. Temperature cycling has no perceptible effect as measured by limit impact velocities. Experiments on firing more than one shot at the same area of armor indicate that several single shots fired in a slow sequence at armor known to resist one such shot do relatively little more damage than one shot, but a machine gun burst of an equal or reduced number of shots hitting the same spot may perforate the armor.

The Jessop steel armor is more resistant, on a weight-for-weight basis, than the 24ST dural armor in thicknesses of dural greater than 0.350-in. In lower thicknesses, the dural is more effective.

The limit impact velocity of $\frac{1}{8}$-in. Doron is about the same as that of $\frac{1}{8}$-in. 24ST dural plate. However, the damage inflicted on Doron by impact of bullets is so great that the maintenance problem involved in using such material in armoring a plane prohibits consideration of its use.

Experiments with five-ply, $1\frac{7}{64}$ in. multiplate glass of the type used around the cockpit of the target airplane showed that this provides adequate protection against the T44 round, since the limit impact velocity of such glass is above 1900 ft/sec. The second of two shots hitting the same small area of the plate with a velocity of approximately 1550 ft./sec. did penetrate the glass, but will not do so if the shots hit as much as $1\frac{1}{2}$ in. apart. A sheet of plexiglass back of five-ply $1\frac{3}{32}$ in. multiplate glass increased its limit impact velocity, as previously defined, by about 300 ft/sec.

C. Propellant

One of the difficulties experienced with the T44 round as loaded in a caliber .30 M1 case was the procurement of a satisfactorily functioning propellant. With the relatively low muzzle velocity of the round (1360 ft./sec.) only a small powder charge (of the order of 0.80 to 0.95 gm) is used and because of the considerable air space, relatively low pressures prevail during the burning of the powder.

The primary requirements of a propellant suitable for use with the T44 bullet were shown to be (i) that it have low position-sensitivity (as regards its location in the case with respect to the primer location), (ii) that it burn relatively completely, and (iii) that in firing the round the modified machine gun function properly. The position sensitivity and approximate amount of unburned powder remaining after firing were determined for a number of different Hercules and Du Pont powders. It was found that the small-grained, fast-burning powders leave little unburned powder in the gun, but that the muzzle velocities obtained with them are quite sensitive to the position of the powder in the case, whereas the large-grained, longer burning powders leave considerable unburned powder in the gun but are relatively position-insensitive. The tests indicate that the requirements of a low position-sensitivity, of proper gun functioning, and of small unburned residue are incompatible in the round as used at present and that some compromises must be made. It was felt that, in the light of these requirements, Du Pont No. 4759 was the best powder of those tested.

Since a wide range of temperatures, varying from room temperature to approximately -50°, are encountered in the use of the T44 round, the average muzzle velocity was determined for nine production lots of T44 rounds at +25°, 0°, and -50°C. The average temperature coefficient between 0° and 25°C for the eight lots loaded by the Western Cartridge Company and St. Louis Ordnance Plant is about 4.5 (ft./sec.)/°C. (This value is considerably higher than that of the one lot tested from the Frankford Arsenal, temperature coefficient, 2.8 [ft./sec.]/°C.)

In firing the T44 production rounds, it was found that the standard deviation of the average muzzle velocity was frequently greater than the acceptable standard deviation of 30 ft/sec. One of the factors that might contribute to the deviation was the variation in moisture content of the Du Pont No. 4759 powder. Since little information was available on the effect of moisture on this particular powder, experiments were carried out to determine (i) the effect of exposure to constant relative humidities on the weight of powder and (ii) the muzzle velocity obtained with powder conditioned two days at a relative humidity of 70%, that subsequent conditioning at 85% relative humidity increases the weight of the powder approximately 0.5%. Firing tests show that the average muzzle velocity may be expected to decrease about 9.8 ft/sec per 0.10% increase in moisture content of the powder.

D. Machine gun

The regular caliber .30 aircraft M2 machine gun will not function as an automatic weapon when the T44 round is fired through it with a muzzle velocity of 1360 ft/sec, since the momentum and muzzle blast are considerably smaller than that of the standard caliber .30 round. In view of this, two modifications of the gun were made, one of which (the piston gun) has been found satisfactory under experimental field conditions. Both types of guns are made automatically operative by use of the gas pressure from the gun barrels.

In the piston gun, the muzzle blast is trapped in a cylinder-piston assembly and the pressure developed gives the barrel and associated parts the required energy for carrying out the automatic operation feature. The rate of fire of the piston gun is influenced by the type of nozzle on the gun but the rate does not vary significantly for small variations in powder charge. The dispersion of shots on a ground target is considerably less with the modified piston gun and T44 round than with the caliber .50 machine gun and caliber .50 ammunition. However, comparable dispersion does occur in air-to-air firing.

Comparison of average muzzle velocities of rounds fired through the new and used gun barrels showed that there was no significant variation in the average muzzle velocity due to difference in barrels.

E. Target airplane

The solution to the problem of firing live ammunition at a real airplane must involve a compromise between the weight of armor that can be put on the target plane and the limit impact velocity of the bullet used against such armor. Therefore, the decision as to the weight and velocity of the bullet and the armoring of the airplane had to be considered simultaneously.

As a first approximation, successful aerial gunnery requires the proper solution of a sighting problem involving the bullet velocity vector, the bomber velocity vector, and the fighter plane velocity vector. It appears that a reasonable facsimile of combat can be obtained by a proper scaling or reduction of all these vectors. The limit of the reduction factor is set by the slowest speed at which it is practical for the bomber to fly. It is necessary also to consider the additional weight of armor permissible on the fighter plane. Finally, the matching conditions between combat and training conditions required a bullet with as high a ballistic coefficient as was practicable.

In general, the most important type of attack from the standpoint of training was the "pursuit-curve" approach of the fighter. In such an attack, if firing was excluded during and after the breakaway, the sections of immediate vulnerability were those surfaces that are visible from a cone defined by a solid angle of 12° and centered along the line of flight of the airplane. The first two types of target planes were armored for use solely with "pursuit-curve" attacks. The first consideration was always the complete protection of the pilot compartment and the most vulnerable parts of the airplane. A secondary consideration was the limitation of damage to a minimum.

Three types of target airplanes have been produced to date. The first was an A-20 airplane armored under the supervision of the Aircraft Laboratory, ATSC, Wright Field. The last two types are modified P-63 airplanes produced by Bell Aircraft Corporation and designated as RP-63C and RP-63G. The details of the armoring and special features of construction of each are discussed in the body of the report. The last type of airplane (RP-63G) was armored so as to be usable for approaches other than those restricted to near pursuit-curve approaches in training and also to allow for the possible higher impact velocities in the B-29 training program. It is not contemplated, however, that continued fire will be directed against the armored airplane from any angle other than those involved in pursuit-curve approaches. [There were three RP models produced, the A, C, and G. Why this report does not recognize the first is unclear. One hundred RP-63As were produced before work began on the RP-63C.]

The only difficulty of significance that has arisen in connection with the armor protection is an occasional failure of the cooling-duct louvers on the RP-63 type airplane to afford adequate protection for the radiators located behind the louvers. A new louver has been designed which presumably will solve the problem. In general, it has not been necessary in field practice to replace any piece of armor because of excessive damage on surfaces where complete protection was intended. As far as is known only three pieces of 1-in. bullet-resistant glass have been replaced because of bullet damage.

An essential feature of the target airplane is a hit-indicator system. The primary features of the system used are as follows:

(1) An electrical generator unit placed on the armor plates so that a potential is developed by the generator when the plate is struck.

(2) An amplifier unit by means of which the generated signal is amplified.

(3) A thyratron-controlled trigger circuit and associated counter, relay, and lamps for signaling to a gunner when a hit has been made and allowing a scoring of such hits.

The installation used in the RP-63C airplanes was furnished, with the exception of the wiring, by the Sperry Gyroscope Company. The gunner signal lamp is mounted in the cannon tube and may be easily seen within a cone of solid angle of about 30° centered about the long axis of the airplane.

The functioning of this installation was somewhat marginal because of spurious triggering and difficulty in proper adjustment of the time-delay relays; therefore considerable work was done toward designing an improved high-indicator system. The American Time Products Company and the Bell Aircraft Corporation have designed amplifiers. At present the amplifier is being furnished by the Bell Aircraft Corporation. Extensive work is underway by several interested agencies on the problem of pickup units. This project has furnished for test purposes two sets of low-cost pickup units, either of which appears to have considerable promise when used with proper filters in the amplifier.

An analysis of the general considerations that will result in reasonable "matching" of the "leads" used with the frangible bullet with those required in combat, shows that with proper adjustment of airplane velocities and sight reticle, and for pursuit-curve attacks, the "match" can be made quite satisfactorily. Theoretical calculations of leads required of gunners firing at the target plane making attacks along curves of pursuit show that the leads, on a "rad" basis, are the same in combat and in training if the adjustments mentioned above are made. The types of attacks considered were lead-pursuit and pure-pursuit attacks against several types of bombers; parallel flight of fighter and bomber; support fire from a bomber formation; and finally fighter-fighter attacks. Data was also included showing the basis of the matching conditions and the impact velocities of the frangible bullets at various instantaneous ranges and "angles-off."

F. Field trials

The essential results obtained to date in field trials of the frangible-bullet technique have been brought together and their implications considered. The first field trials of the frangible bullet were made using the armored A-20 target plane and a YB-40 bomber at Buckingham Army Air Field at Ft. Myers, Florida. These tests proved the general validity of the use of the frangible bullet as a training procedure for aerial gunners. The major part of the remaining field trials of experimental nature have been carried out by the Frangible Bullet Project of the Laredo Army Air Field at Laredo, Texas using the A-20 and the RP-63C target planes. [The RP was an "A" model. The RP-63C was not yet in production.]

Some of the problems which the use of the frangible bullet helped to settle to a reasonable degree follow:

(1) It helped to demonstrate that no single percentage could be chosen as optimum for own-speed settings for compensating sights and that for moderate altitudes (8,000 to 10,000 ft) with average American-type fighters, an own-speed percentage in the vicinity of 65% is more correct than 85%.

(2) It was discovered that the attacking pursuit airplane would not fly in the same pursuit-curve plane of action unless the pursuit airplane speed is the same as that for which its sight had been harmonized. This led to a recommendation that the use of compensating sights in combat be abandoned except for ground strafing.

(3) Tests with fixed optical sights showed that a gunner might be able to learn to use such a device effectively by using "apparent-motion" rules. Considerable instruction with equipment such as the "Henderson's Instructor's Turret" would be required if the gunner were to be made proficient in the use of the optical sight.

(4) With computing sights such as the K-3, K-4, K-15, and G.E., there was definite evidence of gunner learning and the percentage of hits scored was quite satisfactory for training purposes.

(5) It was noted that the gunner student becomes accustomed to fighter attacks and learns to anticipate the fighter's curve and sequence of action. He also learns to range with fair accuracy.

Some of the general limitations of the frangible-bullet technique as brought out by field trials are listed below:

(1) The long time flight of the present frangible bullet, as compared to the time flight of caliber .50 MB ammunition, necessitates large prediction and deflection angles which accentuates the errors of all sights. The increased time of flight also gives the target aircraft more time to depart from a given plane of action.

(2) The frangible bullet T44 would not be stable if shot forward from an airplane going faster than 250 mph true air speed (TAS). This may be of concern in training for future wars. This lack of stability can be remedied to a large degree by decreasing the pitch of the lands in the barrels through which the frangible bullet is fired.

(3) The breaking of tips of the frangible bullets causes some trouble in gun malfunction.

G. Status of frangible-bullet technique

In connection with a discussion of the present status of the frangible bullet in aerial gunnery training a broad analysis of the gunnery problem has been made as a background for the more specialized problem of training. In this analysis the significance is brought out of such elements as the high plane speeds involved, as they relate to the gunner's performance; the bullet's ballistics; and the basis of our knowledge of actual aerodynamic flight of airplanes. The importance of having a sight device or mechanism capable of effective operation in the hands of men of average skill is emphasized in view of the large number—some 150,000—of gunners to be trained annually.

It is pointed out that the requirements that must be met in an adequate training procedure must include opportunity for the gunner to develop the necessary fast reflex responses in a training situation paralleling as closely as possible that in combat. The limitations of some of the prior training methods in the light of these requirements are brought out. The ability of the frangible-bullet technique to fulfill these requirements and its future limitations with the advent of higher plane speeds in combat and of higher bullet velocities are considered. Finally this discussion includes an indication of the possible direction which planning might take to meet this future situation.

The role that the frangible bullet can play in such matters as sight design and modification, study of aerial tactics, particularly in relation to fire from formations, fighter versus fighter gunnery training, and certain naval training problems has been indicated.

The status of the techniques in the training of gunners in bombers as of V-J Day may be summarized as follows:

(1) Bullet production from the small beginning in November 1944 rose to a production capacity of from 40 to 45 million per month in August 1945.

(2) Some 300 armored target airplanes were produced for training by the spring of 1945. Prior to V-J Day 450 additional planes with improved armor had been ordered, all but 30 of these being canceled after V-J Day.

(3) About 11,000 bomber missions, in which some 12 million rounds of frangible-bullet ammunition were fired by student gunners, were flown in the seven gunnery training schools in the United States.

(4) It was stated just prior to V-J Day that all firing from the air in the gunnery program of the Training Command would thereafter be with frangible bullets.

H. Analysis of gunnery skills

In the course of the development of the frangible-bullet technique and its practical application to the training situation, questions frequently arose as to the psychological implications of the "scaling" procedure used in connection with it, both with respect to the modification of sights and the alteration of plane speeds. In an attempt to obtain solid background information that would help in orienting the program in these matters, several series of psychological experiments on the development and analysis of gunnery skills were run with untrained subjects. Tests were made with 61 subjects and involved 350 experimental sessions, representing some 23,000 pointing or tracking trials. The main types of trials included were pointing at a fixed target with variable deflections, tracking a moving target, and pointing with continuously varying deflections at a moving target.

Some of the many points of significance for the general gunnery training problem brought out by these investigations are the following:

(1) The desirability of some method, such as the instructor's or "slave" turret, for providing the student with a knowledge of his errors at the time of training.

(2) An evaluation of the relative contribution to the final overall firing errors attributable in a given sight mechanism to, say, tracking versus ranging, should be based upon performance after training of gunners in the use of the mechanism. This would indicate that if it were possible to choose between automatic radar control of one of the other of these functions in the sight, this decision should be reached on the basis of trials by gunners trained on the basic sight mechanism and the results of such trials should be weighed along with the engineering and design considerations.

(3) Skill in tracking once acquired through training seems to be retained for a period of at least six weeks. On the other hand there was a lack of retention of the skill acquired in the case where the student was trained to point a machine gun quickly at a target and at the same time give accurately a predetermined lead deflection away from the target.

Because of the limitations in terms of number of subjects involved in these experiments the foregoing conclusions must be regarded as preliminary in nature. However, they illustrate the possibilities of obtaining information of prime importance to a gunnery training program from psychological experiments on student gunners provided these are carried out with test equipment closely paralleling the gunnery situation itself. Such information should have important implications not only for the training program itself but in relation to such matters as the design and choice of sight mechanisms.

I. Princeton tests of characteristics of several types of bullets

In view of the desirability of having as broad a basis as possible for selection of the type of frangible bullet to be used in production, experiments for this purpose were carried out at the Princeton University Station of Division 2 in addition to those carried out at Duke University.

The Princeton Laboratory made velocity-loss and time-of-flight measurements for six types of caliber .30 bullets to determine their suitability for use in the frangible-bullet technique for the training of flexible gunners. One of the bullets tested had the shape of caliber .30 M1906 ball and was similar to the T44 bullet in current use. Only one of the other five bullets tested showed a drag significantly less than the T44. This bullet, which had a secant ogive and boattail, showed a marked advantage over the T44 only for velocities below about 1200 ft./sec. However, this is the velocity range of interest as the T44 is fired at a muzzle velocity of 1360 ft./sec. A determination of stability factors are [sic] necessary to indicate more clearly whether a bullet of this type offers a distinct advantage over the type in use.

The Princeton University Station has also done some preliminary work on a caliber .50 frangible bullet. The ballistic coefficient G_6 of this bullet was found to be approximately 0.25 which would give an acceptable "match" with the combat case for types of attack other than pursuit curve. However, data obtained for the limit impact velocity of the caliber .50 bullet against 24ST dural showed that it would not be safe to fire this ammunition at the present type of armored planes when using a muzzle velocity as high as 1360 ft./sec.

J. Accessory equipment

It became obvious in connection with the broad training program being developed for use with the T44 frangible bullet that the development or modification of several accessory pieces of equipment would help to improve the training. Thus, Major H. I. Henderson pointed out that it would be desirable for the instructor to be able to criticize the student at the actual time an attack is made. The best way to do this seemed to be through the development of an instructor's or "slave" turret driven by the student's turret.

It was decided that the most immediate solution of this problem would result from the adaptation to this purpose of the Central-station Fire-Control System developed by the General Electric Company and used on the B-29 airplanes. In this adaptation the gunner's turret controlled another turret in which an instructor might observe the action of the student while firing at an attacking plane. An upper-rear turret of the B-29 was modified so that it could carry an instructor and would reproduce the movements in both azimuth and elevation of a Martin turret which would be operated by a student gunner. The Martin turret was fitted with the necessary selsyn generators to enable it to drive the instructor's turret into proper alignment.

An NB-A gunsight mounted in a deflectometer was attached to the sight yoke of the instructor's turret. A camera was mounted so that it was possible to make photographs and visual observations simultaneously.

Measurements were made to determine the accuracy with which this instructor's turret followed the driving turret. These measurements indicated that the accuracy of alignment of the two turrets was such that no significant errors in the evaluation of the student gunner would result.

Further preliminary work has been done in this general connection on arranging a selsyn-controlled range system so that the range setting on a computing sight in the Martin turret is reproduced on a computing sight mounted in the instructor's turret. Such a system should also prove of value in the B-29 training program.

Appendix B

The Bell fighters*

Model	Number Procured	Gross Wt. (Pounds)	Dimensions		Engine[1]		Top Speed
			Span	*Length*	*Model*	*Horsepower*	
XP-39	1	6204	35′ 10″	28′ 8″	V-1710- 17	1150	390
YP-39A[2]	(1)	7250	34′ 0″	30′ 2″	V-1710- 31	1150	384
XP-39B[3]	(1)	6450	34′ 0″	29′ 9″	V-1710- 37	1090	379
P-39C[4]	(80)	7180	34′ 0″	30′ 2″	V-1710- 35	1150	379
P-39D	863	8200	34′ 0″	30′ 2″	V-1710- 35	1150	368
XP-39E[5]	3	8918	35′ 10″	31′ 11″	V-1710- 47	1350	386
P-39F[6]	229	7500	34′ 0″	30′ 2″	V-1710- 35	1150	368
P-39J	25	8260	34′ 0″	30′ 2″	V-1710- 59	1100	360
P-39K	210	8400	34′ 0″	30′ 2″	V-1710- 63	1325	368
P-39L	250	8500	34′ 0″	30′ 2″	V-1710- 63	1325	365
P-39M	240	8400	34′ 0″	30′ 2″	V-1710- 83	1200	360
P-39N	2095	8200	34′ 0″	30′ 2″	V-1710- 85	1200	379
P-39Q	4905	8300	34′ 0″	30′ 2″	V-1710- 85	1200	385
XP-63[7]	2	7525	38′ 4″	32′ 8″	V-1710- 47	1325	407
XP-63A	1	7705	38′ 4″	32′ 8″	V-1710- 93	1325	401
P-63A	1725	10000	38′ 4″	32′ 8″	V-1710- 93	1325	400
RP-63A	100	8300	38′ 4″	32′ 8″	V-1710- 93	1325	400+
P-63C	1227	10700	38′ 4″	32′ 8″	V-1710-117	1325	410
RP-63C	200	8500	38′ 4″	32′ 8″	V-1710-117	1325	400+
P-63D[8]	1	11100	39′ 2″	32′ 8″	V-1710-109	1425	437
P-63E[9]	13	11200	39′ 2″	32′ 8″	V-1710-109	1425	410
P-63F	1	11500	39′ 2″	32′ 8″	V-1710-135	1425	400+
RP-63G	32	11500	39′ 2″	32′ 8″	V-1710-135	1425	400+

NOTE: Figures in parentheses not included in total procured.

**U. S. Army Aircraft* by James C. Fahey. Copyright © 1946 by James C. Fahey. Ships and Aircraft, publisher.

Notes:
[1]Allison, V-12, liquid cooled.
[2]YP-39 with altitude engine, no turbo.
[3]XP-39 with engine change and no turbo.
[4]Originally designated P-45; sixty became P-39Ds. Not included in chart are 645 Bell Model 14s, a modification of the P-39C originally ordered by England.
[5]With laminar flow wing and fittings for Continental IV-1430-1 engine. Test bed for XP-63.
[6]Same as P-39D except for engine change.
[7]Same as XP-39E except for increased wing dimensions.
[8]Revised design with engine change and bubble canopy.
[9]Same as P-63D but with new prop, radio and standard cockpit canopy.

Bibliography

Books

Bowyer, Chaz. *Guns In The Sky.* New York: Charles Scribner's Sons, 1979.

Brown, K. S., Lt. Col. USAF. *United States Army and Air Force Fighters 1916-1961.* London: Harleyford Publications, Ltd., 1962.

Burchard, John E., ed. *Rockets, Guns and Targets.* Boston: Little, Brown and Company, 1948.

Fahey, J. D. *U. S. Army Aircraft.* 1st ed. Falls Church, VA: Ships and Aircraft, 1946.

Farley, Edward J. *U.S. Army Air Force Fighter Planes P-1 to F-107,* Third Edition. Aero Publishers, 1961.

Graven, Wesley F. and Cate, James L., ed. *The Army Air Forces in World War II, Vol. VI: Men and Planes.* Chicago: The University of Chicago Press, 1955.

Jablonski, Edward. *Airwar.* Garden City, N.Y.: Doubleday & Company, Inc., 1971.

Munson, Kenneth G. *Aircraft of World War Two.* London: Ian Allen, Ltd.

Musciano, Walter A. *Messerschmitt Aces.* New York: Arco Publishing, Inc., 1982.

Shores, Christopher. *Duel For The Sky.* Garden City, N.Y., Doubleday & Company, Inc., 1985.

Swanborough, F. G. *United States Military Aircraft Since 1909.* London and New York: Putnam, 1963.

Wagner, Ray. *American Combat Planes.* Garden City, N.Y.: Doubleday & Co., 1968.

Magazine Articles

"Brittle Bullets Give Air Gunners Combat Practice." *Popular Science,* May 1945.

"Shooting Doesn't Hurt." *Science Newsletter,* March 31, 1945.

"Sparring Partner." The Ordnance Sergeant, May 1945.

Vanderschmidt, Fred. "Air Forces' New Frangible Bullet Teaches Gunners With Live Targets." *Newsweek,* March 19, 1945.

Scientific Reports and Articles

Eisenhart, Churchill. "Technical Aspects of Frangible Projectiles for Flexible Gunnery Training." *AMG Report No. 93,* November 19, 1943.

Hedlund, Gustav A. "Frangible Bullets and Aerial Gunnery." *AMP Memo No. 167.1M,* July 1945.

Hobbs, Nicholas, ed. "Psychological Research on Flexible Gunnery Training." *Report No. 11,* U. S. Government Printing Office, 1947.

MacLane, Saunders. "Frangible Bullets." AMG Report No. 321, December 2, 1944.

"Deformable Projectiles for Flexible Gunnery Training." Report No. A-210, Research Project No. P2-105, OSRD No. 1788. Princeton University and Duke University: September 1943.

"Ordnance and Terminal Ballistics," Vol. 12, U.S. Office of Scientific Research & Development, NDRC, 1946.

"The Frangible Bullet for Use in Aerial Gunnery Training." U.S. Office of Scientific Research & Development, NDRC, 1946.

Official Military Publications

"Flexible Gunnery Training in the AAF." Army Assistant Chief of Staff, Intelligence.

"History of Army Air Forces Training Command and its Predecessor Commands, January 1, 1939 - V-J Day." Hq. AAF Training Command, June 15, 1946.

"History of Army Air Forces Flexible Gunnery School, Las Vegas Army Air Field" with associated Las Vegas AAF unit histories, July 1, 1944 - March 31, 1946.

"History of Harlingen Army Air Field" with associated Harlingen AAF unit histories, March 1 - October 31, 1945.

"History of Laredo Army Air Field" with associated Laredo AAF unit histories, September 1, 1944 - December 1945.

"History of Tyndall Army Air Field" with associated Tyndall AAF unit histories, March 1, 1945 - February 28, 1946.

"History of Yuma Army Air Field" with associated Yuma AAF unit histories, January 1, 1945 - June 30, 1945.

"Organizational History, 3533rd AAF Base Unit, Sperry Gyroscope Company." September 1, 1944 - August 31, 1945.

"Photographic Assessment of RP-63 Aircraft and Pursuit Attacks, 1945." U. S. Naval Air Test Center, Patuxent River, Md., Armament Test Division.

"Small Arms and Small Arms Ammunition," Vol. 2. Record of Army Ordnance Research and Development, Office of Chief of Ordnance, January 1946.

"Station History, Kingman Army Air Field," with associated Kingman AAF unit histories, July 1, 1944 - September 30, 1945.

"Suitability Test of Armored RP-63C Airplane and the T44 Bullet as Testing and Training Equipment." Report by US Army Air Forces Board, Orlando, Florida.